POETRY NOW

WEST COUNTRY 1996

Edited by Andrew Head

First published in Great Britain in 1996 by
POETRY NOW
1-2 Wainman Road, Woodston,
Peterborough, PE2 7BU

SB ISBN 1 85731 652 5

FOREWORD

Although we are a nation of poetry writers we are accused of not reading poetry and not buying poetry books: after many years of listening to the incessant gripes of poetry publishers, I can only assume that the books they publish, in general, are books that most people do not want to read.

Poetry should not be obscure, introverted, and as cryptic as a crossword puzzle: it is the poet's duty to reach out and embrace the world.

The world owes the poet nothing and we should not be expected to dig and delve into a rambling discourse searching for some inner meaning.

The reason we write poetry (and almost all of us do) is because we want to communicate: an ideal; an idea; or a specific feeling. Poetry is as essential in communication, as a letter; a radio; a telephone, and the main criteria for selecting the poems in this anthology is very simple: they communicate.

Faced with hundreds of poems and a limited amount of space, the task of choosing the final poems was difficult and as editor one tries to be as detached as possible (quite often editors can become a barrier in the writer-reader exchange) acting as go between, making the connection, not censoring because of personal taste.

In this anthology over two hundred and forty poems are presented to the reader for their enjoyment.

The poetry is written on all levels; the simple and the complex both having their own appeal.

The success of this collection, and all previous *Poetry Now* anthologies, relies on the fact that there are as many individual readers as there are writers, and in the diversity of styles and forms there really is something to please, excite, and hopefully, inspire everyone who reads the book.

CONTENTS

MY DOG CALLED FLUFFY

There's a mass of fur on the floor,
It's yellow and a bit hard.

Mom's hair's brown, dad's is black,
Jason's is a ginger nut!
Can't be theirs or mine,
To whot can it be?
I'm not quite sure.

Then mom whalks in and says,
'Oh, you've discovered it,
How do you like our nice new pet?'
'But mom, where's its eyes, shining bright?
Where's its tail, like a kite?'

Mom picks it up and parts the hair,
'Here's its eyes shining bright,
Here's its tail like a kite.'

'What's her name, what's she called?'
'Fluffly, that's her name,'
Because she's like a mass of fur upon the floor.

Emma Manley

THE OLD OAK

There lies a great old English Oak
Which once was planted there
By gentle hands of country folk
For everyone to share
But now its arms are broken,
It's head lies on the ground,
Its heart is just a chip of wood
That's splintered all around.

Shirley Noreen Jacks

MOUNTAIN - YOU AND I

Mountains, moulded by the hands
of the divine sculptor.
Battered and shaped by nature's relentless power
to become an epitome of God's steadfastness.

Created to raise our hearts and minds -
above the mundane incidents of everyday living
to a realisation of the power and majesty of our creator.

I gaze on you and am filled
with an awesome wonder of God.

You give me comfort in the thought
that the God who fashioned and moulded you
is doing the same thing in me.

Together, mountain, you and I give
praise to the God of creation.

Frances Squires

OLD AND YOUNG

Once I was young, blithe of spirit, strong of limb, hair rich in colour,
Now I am growing old, wrinkles, grey hair,
My body, my mind, play tricks one against the other.

When you look at me what do you see?
Someone past their prime?
At the close of their time?
Look again, deep into my eyes,
You will see,
Not furrowed brow, infirmity,
But a young person as you are now and I used to be.

J E Light

DAVID'S WALK

Whilst musing amongst those beauteous rides
Of Rhododendrons and Azaleas
Reflecting on Herculean strides
And on our dismal failures

I watched the firmament turn inside out
to paint peacock blue there on the earth
Fast took away a nagging doubt
made me aware of man's true worth

A million bells pealed out the news
That in the end wild nature rules
And only she of a myriad hues
Can give direction to hapless fools

Only those dank, owl - light woods
And grasslands splashed with poppy red
Can cast off man's black faceless hoods
And help him rise from pains last bed

I took those footsteps then with pride
A smile chased across my sun - drenched face
And I walked along that sky - splashed ride
to the starting gate of my next race

For though our achievements can scarce compare
there are those who are allied with nature still
Following in the footsteps of love and care
of those who would rather save than kill

It is folly to set ourselves apart
Seeing natural law a separate thing
For inside each one of us the heart
Beats time with nature here this spring.

David W Robinson

AFRICAN CHILDREN

Children are crying in Africa
Silent tears roll down their cheeks
All they want is food and comfort
They haven't had that for weeks

Children are sighing in Africa
The sun beats down from above
The land is dusty and barren
They miss the ones that they love

Children are dying in Africa
Their eyes are so big and so scared
Tummies are swollen, and limbs are thin
If only more people cared

Children are lying in Africa
They lie on the hard, cracked ground
Nothing thrives and nothing survives
All you hear is a whimpering sound

Children are crying in Africa
They know so much suffering and pain
No food, no beds and no cuddles
Will they ever be happy again?

Jillian Margaret Campbell

A LEGACY

Tell me *old man*, tell me how you used to look for miles
across fields and see masses of daffodils gently moving their
trumpet-like heads in the breeze, unfolding a yellow carpet
as far as the eye could see.

Tell me of the fish, the trout and the salmon, that used to leap
up river and jump the cool clear rapids.
Tell me *old man* tell me.

Tell me of the trees that sprouted green leaves, and then in the Autumn changed to many different colours before falling to the ground, where you could wade knee deep in this carpet of leaves that seemed to be a kaleidoscope.

What of the birds with their bright coloured plumage flying in the rays of the sun, only to disappear into the fields of barley and corn, and then appear again from this sea of light brown mass of crops in all their majesty with food for their young.

Tell me *old man*, tell me. Explain to me what a Whale and a Seal looked like before they were all killed off. I know nothing of these things, and I shall never see them.

Before our world was polluted and turned into a dust bowl, what was it like? Tell me *old man*, tell me.

Joey Caple

BREDWARDINE

After much chattering and dashing about
The stream settles down and quietly joins the river
Slips clear over stones to lose itself in the indifferent mass

Framed under an arch of the bridge
A family of swans fits the picture
Colour-colded for age, white old, grey new.

Up in the churchyard Kilvert's grave is too white
The urn bare of flowers, wish I'd brought some
Something of his spirit around the seat under the yew.
It seems Kilvert died of marriage.

Inside a theological library offers a book
Entitled 'Creative Pain.'
I go out past the font with its witch-proof cover
I can't believe in any of it.

Sally Weinhardt

SLIPS AWAY - HYSTERICAL
(or a writers' agony!)

Waiting for inspiration
I know to be in vain
clouds are slipping by
the sun, replaced with rain.

Hours too, have flown
barely I notice their passing
extensions, endlessly rooted
inner vision, pitifully glassing.

Pit in stomach darkens
O, great yawning chasm
while chaotic thoughts are chased
discarded with sarcasm.

Still, can't let go now
the day closes, night awakes
my world slips into silence
in ignorance of physical aches.

Mellifluous incomprehensibilities
skate around, decreasing circle
there'll be no devastating truths
sanity slips away . . . *Hysterical!*

Sue Jackson

THE OLD FISHERMAN

What is he thinking, that old fisherman?
As he wanders by the river, day after endless day,
Whiling the unimportant hours away;
The gulls wheel close above his head, indifferently,
To them he is just part of their familiar scenery.

6

Gone are the energies of youth and all his friends,
No lave nets needed now for him to him to make or mend,
Seldom seen, the quick silver flash of salmon the summer sun,
Sensitive, undisputed king of river fish, they could not alter,
To withstand the increased pollution of the water.

So nothing changes in his life now, but the ever-changing sands,
Time is not his master now, and no-one makes demands,
His face is tranquil as a tranquil tide, as day after day,
He wiles the halcyon summer months away,
In his own simple, chosen way.

The long sun-drenched, summer days have gone, the old man too,
Grey winter mists obscure the river from my view,
Perhaps he is still there, somewhere beyond the river's bend,
In happy reunion with his friends,
Eternity for him is a prolific fishing day that never ends.

Jennifer Lord

BOSNIA - HOMAGE TO THE FALLEN

A daily bulletin renews itself
                    with awful news,
Broken bodies queuing for bread, that
Staff of life, we all strive for.
Our existence is justified by the
                    Nurturing of seeds
Humanity grows as nature thrusts
                    with her mighty
                              atom,
Big eared men listen to the sounds
                    of distant drums,
Territories become extinct, yet the guns
                    are never silent,
Names and boundaries, meaning less causes,
Innocents pay for these worthless dreams.

Olivia Hicks

7

THIS EMPTY HOUSE

Hollow memories fill this empty house
Lifeless rooms have died with time
once the laughter of children lived here
once that laughter was mine

Creaking floorboards
Lay dirty and bare
The sunbeams smile through splintered panes
Clean square on the wall
A picture hung there
The picture had no name

Gaping fireplace
A smoke stained room
Once the heart of this house
So grand
It beats no more
the home is dead
Its death was never planned

My old home now is but an empty house
I feel I've lost a lifelong friend
You saw me grow
From my beginning
I see you at your end

Shayne Meredith

PAST GLOUCESTER SOMEWHERE

River, fields, hills and dales, Avon has them all
A pretty county newly formed and soon about to fall.

From Gloucestershire to the North to Somerset in the West,
People know these counties and think they are the best.

Avon where is that? They ask exactly on the map
Somewhere by Wales perhaps just filling up a gap.

But local people know its worth and proudly walk its streets,
Knowing that around each bend lay even more treats.

It's part of a bigger picture *The West Country* as it's known
It's produce known world wide Cider, cheese, pasties and scones.

The whole area is beautiful and bathed in history,
It's why so many people holiday here it's really no mystery.

So let us stop and think awhile and contemplate this thought,
Beauty, peace and tranquillity just cannot be bought.

It's where my heart and soul is, it's where I want to be
There's nowhere quite like it, it's home enough for me.

Jane Fletcher

WINTER CHILL

The wind blows hard, the clouds from the sky
The cauldron boils and breaks
The white water winds like a viper,
Cutting through the mountain side like a disease.

Fast as lightening, furious and free,
It runs through the mountain like blood through a vein,
And it drips from the caves as silver rain,
Falling softly on the moss like snow
As the rain falls in blankets.
The old man leans forwards into the wind
As his never ending hike continues into the night
His body numb and white,
Like the sheep that shuffle from hill to hill.
As the cold air bites like an untamed beast
The sheep tonight shall be his feast.

Andrew MacCallum

ALIVE

As I part the curtains, the light is blinding.
It gushes and overflows
Like fresh mountain spring water .
My sleep-soaked eyes feel drowned;
They flounder and blink to adjust.
The room, once dove-like and grey,
Has been repainted rich and bright and gold:
The dove has flown.

Thirsty for more, I reach, reach to the sun.
As the window yawns, the air slides;
It runs across my arm, a ribbon of silk.
Endless sound arrives at my ears, and enters.
An orchestra strikes up in my head,
Soft and pleasant
Birdsong, wind in leaves, trickling stream.

An elixir of scent blesses my nostrils,
Encircles my face and neck.
Rain and dew-drenched earth, wood and leaf,
Rose, privet, grasses:
Sweet air.

The entirety of my humanity and senses
Are instantaneously addressed; called to attention.
I am alive . . .
And this day I will live.

Gemma Parkes

THE THING THAT FLEW THROUGH THE WINDOW

A thing flew through the window,
With orange and green polka dot,
Vein ridden pterodactyl wings,
And its breath was hot!

'Strewth! Somebody kill it,'
The vicar loud did shout,
As hot tea upon his lap was spilt,
And rock cakes strewn about.

With unsophisticated vault,
Mrs Jones cleared the settee,
I think it will be some time before,
The vicar calls again for tea.

Rock cakes on floor in disarray,
Butter on the wall,
Vicar's temper gone to pot,
Oh! The anguish of it all.

'Can I have that thing back mum?
You know, the one with polka dots,
I've just put new batteries in,
And it's a toy of which I think a lot.'

T H Lord

THE EVER LASTING LIGHT

The light in our lives is forever burning, shining, glowing
Helping us in our daily life,
Sometimes it flickers side by side showing us that we are doing wrong,

If we go off our tracks he brings us back again,
Then the light will put us right again,
Then we call out to our Lord,
Help us for our strength to carry on,
Guide us we pray with the light that comes from our Lord,
Help us Lord day by day.

For as long as we love we will always have that light,
If you wish to follow him,
Guiding, showing us the right path he leads the way.

Cherokee Hamilton

TEME-SIDE MEMORIES

When I heard your voice softly speaking to me
Images reappeared of seasons long past,
Many were the pleasant hours we shared
In your cottage cocooned by trees,
Close by the murmuring Teme.

I remember seeing the trees from your window,
Black limbs interlaced against the sky,
In my mind's eye, branches heavy-laden,
Fresh pale green leaves unfurling
in that sweet month of June.

On those summer days of seasons long past
We roamed the woodlands and meadows,
Through rippling fields of yellow grass,
Resting beside the meandering Teme
Saw Kingfishers flashing by.

In that shimmering heat at summer's height
No rustle of wind stirred the leaves,
Together in the sun-scorched grass,
Bodies bronzed by the burning sun,
Idyllic those golden hours.

At summer's end we picked ripened fruit,
Our fingers stained purple by juice,
You picked swollen, succulent berries,
And turning towards me with a smile
Pressed fruit between my lips.

Hush of winter-time passed, spring awoke anew,
Alone I longed for time that had passed,
But you had vanished like melting snow,
When I heard your voice from afar
I knew you remembered too.

Betty Mealand

SHE-DEVIL

You came from nowhere,
spite flashing,
Words slashing,
Venom pouring.
Your words rained blows
I cringed.
You remained unchecked, eyes flashing.
You slashed my image,
You bruised my soul.
Were you satisfied?
I'll never know.

Nicola Stait

IT'S OVER

It's over now, it's hard to believe
My love I didn't want to leave.
I had to say goodbye
But you didn't see me cry
I must now let you go
But I must keep trying
Though inside I am dying
They say time will heal
But only time will tell.

Now it's over
Will I ever feel whole
When will this empty space heal
I wish I could see you again
Can't rid myself of this pain
So forever I will dream
You don't know just what you mean
But my love I know it's over.

Sheridan Perrie

THE POSTMAN

A pale sun shone on snowdrops by the hedge
Robins and Sparrows fight over crumbs on the window ledge
      Maggie gazed up the lane
But the postman waved as he passed by again.

Blossoms on the orchard trees
The garden alive with the buss of bees
      By the hedge Maggie looks up the lane
But the postman calls 'Hello' and passes by again.

The Autumn leaves of red and gold.
The mornings and evenings getting cold.
      Maggie stands by the window gazing up the lane
But the postman passes with a wave once again.

In the hearth the fire glows
The wall adorned with holly boughs.
Down the lane the postman comes to call
      Maggie meets him in the hall
At last a card from far away
To say thinking of you mum on Christmas Day.

Vera Harding-Miles

DO YOU WONDER?

Do you wonder where it all went wrong?
Can't you find the strength to carry on?
Why are things so bad, why is life so sad?
Where is all the joy you should have had?

Have you ever stopped to wonder why
Best things in life just pass you by?
You've lost a lot, and now you've got
No fight left in you any more.

14

Do you want to know the things I know?
Do you want to know which way to go?
I was just like you, lost and weary too,
Until God showed me what to do.

You've no need to wonder any more
You can find, like me, what you're looking for
A constant friend, until the end
And He's there for each and every one.

Now you'll see the beauty of the days
Love of life will be yours always
You'll find your peace, and great release
So don't you waste another day.

Josie Edwards

NOVEMBER POPPIES

The language of flowers is filled with the balm
　　Of natures' great beauty for all.
But, one flower alone serves to fracture the calm,
　　'Tis the poppy - slender and tall.
In infertile regions with limited yields
　　They flourish in billowing waves;
As in mud twixt the trenches of Flanders' Fields
　　Where they grew on the makeshift graves.
Each soft crimson petal belies the cruel fact
　　Of the price mankind has to pay;
In lives ended. . . broken. . . to furnish wars' pact
　　In the crudest possible way.
So sour the aroma. . . so vivid the hue
　　Of this red funeral pall;
To ever remember . . . and pay reverence due,
　　The November poppy bids all.

Eric Wilks

15

SIAN

'It's now or never'
She says as she races
along the road.
Fighting for space on the pavement,
filled with so many.
Each with its voice and brain.
But hers is different, her mind
is photographic and her opinions
are endless.
Keep pushing, each door
that slams shut is an incentive.
Impulse taken to the extreme.
Don't slow down,
or that opportunity is missed.
Her talking is as creative
as her writing,
both demand so much attention.
Each breath is her rest.
'It's now or never'
echoes in her shadows.

Aimee Chuter

ODE TO THAT SOMETHING

What is that something which attracts me to you,
Where does it come from, I have not a clue.
Perhaps it is the smell of your scent and deep throated laugh,
Your sparkling nature, when acting so daft.

What is that something, I cannot point out,
How do you think and what are you about?
So often I wonder and muse with my thoughts,
As I question the logic to my silent retorts.

16

What is that something that drives me so mad?
Perhaps it is your passion which makes me act bad,
Or soft tender kisses that entice me to bed.
Though it could be those thoughts rooted deep in your head.

What is that something so strong and so sure,
The intense feeling it creates that makes me crave more.
You like to play games with illusions I so often miss,
Sometimes I cannot comprehend, but would never dismiss.

What is that something that increases with pleasure.
It is unique and un-recognisable with no scale of measure!

Louise Perry

ANOTHER VALENTINE'S DAY

Another Valentine's Day:
Looped wool mat, bare,
and the letters *Welcome Home* looked up,
no envelopes with love messages inside,
not even a gas bill coloured brown,
just large red letters;
Welcome Home looked up and stared;
the looped wool mat lay bare.

A day of wishing, wondering,
a card of love could be there
lying flat on the looped wool mat,
with large red letters saying *Welcome Home*
joy would be felt,
that somebody cared.
No,
Not this Valentine's day;
the looped wool mat lay bare,
and the letters *Welcome Home*
gave that vacant stare.

Paul Felton

THE FIELD

Have you a story to unfold
Lying there, so large and bold,
So innocent, you face the sky
And left alone, you'd rather lie.

You've seen life's story from the start
And often, played a major part,
Where, battles many, have been fought
And destiny, so oft-times wrought.

What tales hide you, within your sod
Ay! Tales so noble; and others, odd,
Legends of famine, and of gold
Tales of life, both young and old.

How many lovers, in the past
Have dallied there, for loves repast,
Where, life begins, amongst the kine
But more my chance, than by design.

Where are the treasures, from the past
That lie within your girth, so vast,
Hidden there, from greedy eyes
A bank-vault; in a poor mans guise.

What memories have you in your earth
In bones of men, that saw no mirth,
The souls of villeins, worked to die
And always; it's the wives that cry.

And, what's you future going to be?
- As in the past; I'll guarantee!

G C Garbutt (Bristol)

18

BATH OLIVER

'It does annoy me so,' the old man muttered,
to see Bath Abbey so memorial-cluttered.'
- 'Hold on, Dad,' his fellow-tourist reasoned:
'Some of it's rubbish - but much isn't.
This monument you're standing under now
conceals a stirring story, let me tell you how.
Above, you see a plume that's carved in stone;
below, the tablet tells us about one
William Oliver, physician to the Fleet -
but what he was before, the text dares not repeat
except in code: 'his country's miseries
call'd for a deliverer' - but which this is,
Monmouth or King William, it carefully won't say:
the plume above is what gives the game away . . .

'In 1685 Duke Monmouth reeled
from terminal defeat on Sedgemoor Field.
As Kirke's Lambs closed in for the kill,
one man stayed loyal to the Duke - young Will:
'Let's swap our plumes and promptly disappear
in opposite directions. That way, Sir,
you can escape to Wales, and so to France.'
The doctor led the King a merry dance,
sharing his coach with Judge Jeffreys' clerk
(no doubt keeping the Duke's plume dark).
But Monmouth didn't take his medicine.
He wandered east; was dragged out of a rhine.
The doctor would refuse for 30 years
to make official *which* had been his wars . . .'

'Bless his brave spirit! Where's the real plume?'
- 'Stuck in a zoo until the day of Doom.'

Adrian Risdon

19

MICHAEL

'There's something in your face Michael, I've seen it all the day,
There's something that wasn't there, when first you went away.'

'It's just the army life mother, the drill, the left, the right
That puts the stiffening in your spine, and locks the jaw uptight.'

'There's something in your eyes Michael, and how they stare and stare,
You're looking at me now my boy, as if I wasn't there.'

'It's the sights I've seen mother, the sights that come and come,
A bit of broken bloody pulp, that used to be your chum.'

'There's something in your head Michael, that makes you wake at night,
And often when I hear you move, I tremble in my fright.'

'It's the man I killed mother, a mother's son like me,
It seems he's always haunting, he'll never let me be.'

'But maybe he was bad Michael, maybe it was right?
To kill the enemy you hate in fair and honest fight.'

'I did not hate him mother, he never did me no harm
I think he was a lad like me, that worked upon farm.'

'Then what's it all about Michael, and why did you have to go,
A quiet peaceful lad like you, and we were happy so.'

'It's them that's up above mother, it's them that sits and rules
We have to fight the wars they make, it's us that are the fools.'

'Then what will be the end Michael, and what's the use I say,
Of fighting? If whoever wins, it's us that's got to pay.'

'Oh it will end mother, when lads like him and me,
That sweat to feed the ones above, decide that we'll be free.'

'And when will that day be Michael, and when will the fighting cease,
And simple lads that work and toil the land, will live and love in peace.'

'It's coming nearer mother, it's nearer everyday, that all who earn
Their honest bread, in every land and soil, will join the Brotherhood of Man
The comradeship of toil, when we the workers all decide, what are
We fighting for, then we shall end this stupid folly, this devils crime!
                    War

Danny Price

A SOLDIER'S CONSCIENCE

Life can be bad, but it's invariably good,
Thirty years have proved this to me,
I've travelled the world by land,
And I've travelled the world by sea.
As a soldier I was taught the art to kill,
But I'd rather let life live,
'Cos all the killing, and hurting, and maiming,
No-one can ever forgive.

I was taught the art of killing
By a soldier, much older than me;
'You kill him, or he'll kill you,
That's the way it'll always be'
Yes, folks are too busy killing,
To know what's really true,
And that's for you to be nice to me,
And for me to be nice to you.

I've had bullets rip past my torso,
I've shot back and been closer than he
I've watched his hand grip at his leg
Where his kneecap used to be.
My bullet has shattered the limb,
That nature made with skill:
As I see the blood, I see the soldier,
Who long ago taught me to kill!

Dave Carpenter

IN MEMORY
OF THOMAS KEN 1637-1711

From Longleat House along the drive they bear,
All that remains on earth of him who bore,
True loyalty to that he did so firmly hold,
To be the will of Him, he did in life adore.

At Weymouth's house your sojourn now must end,
And six poor men now bring your body hence.
Ride on brave Christian Saint, ride on towards your home,
Where Christ in glory bids you gather round his throne.

But wait, where wend these six poor men their path?
Surely to Andrew's church in Wells they come,
Bringing their brother to the place where he belongs,
To lie at peace amongst the noblest in the land.

Yet these are not the streets of Wells they take,
But hilly, rough and cobbled Gentle Street,
And here they place amongst the humble parish folk,
He who once bore the noble title, Bath and Wells.

To Frome your final resting place they come,
Your poor remains they carry to St John's;
No lavish tomb within it's ancient courts for you,
Here you must lie without, scarce noticed by the throng.

But I remember when St John's I pass,
Or stand at Heaven's Gate in Longleat Park,
And praise with you the One from whom all blessings flow,
The one most blessed Father, Son and Holy Ghost.

David Jukes

ATTAINMENT

Great is the strength from which my healing soul imparts
born of subterfuge, courage, pervading my heart
Grief stricken magnitude shrouded in time
an endless abundance of rhythm and rhyme.

Oh speak to me, speak to me, hear what I say
as wonders abound at the end of the day
An inner peace from my sorrows fulfil
time ridden energies, bereft and at will.

Cautions of wonderment, silence is found
inept and fastidious and lulled to the ground
No predators here to lie or deceive,
but joyous attainment, uncluttered, with ease.

Janice Honeybourne

MIRROR IMAGE

I saw you in the mirror, the hatred in your eyes,
I know you really love her, wish she was in your bed
Her soft gentle beauty calls you
Her love she freely gives
You ache to be there with her
For me not to exist.

I saw you in the mirror, the hatred in your eyes
My looks start to offend you, my dress to irritate
My voice, my walk, my breathing,
My life you wish would end.

But we have not the courage to face up to
such trauma, so I turn round from the mirror
Smile a sad and lonely smile
Husband and wife together living out a lie.

Rosemary Jennings

THE BARN OWLS

They sweep the land with snowy, silent wings,
Which speak of love, and danger, and dark things:
Conscious always, each one of the other,
The twilight hours provide their cover -
The hunting pair wander far and wide,
Majestic, ghost-like, side by side -
At once so graceful, sinister, powerful, strange
The evening peace their secrets claims.

Susan Fenelon

ODE FOR THE ROAD

One cold day in the winter,
David thought he'd buy a car,
one to take his family out in,
see the sights both near and far.

One fine morning in the evening,
David thought he'd buy a bus,
one that was in fine condition,
four bald tyres and full of rust.

Yesterday after tomorrow,
the morn before the night before,
David though he'd buy a carthorse,
big enough to carry four

In the stable of the garage,
between the bus and family car,
sleeps poor Dobbin, David's carthorse,
don't you think it's quite bizarre?

Joe Caruso

24

CLAIR

Oh, she was a misery, Clair
always thinking life unfair.
Moaning, groaning all day long,
singing a dirge never a song.

Nagging here, harping there,
seeing problems everywhere.
She was always full of woe,
never high, only low.

Hubby tried the best he could,
smile at him she never would.
She'd often turn to him, and say,
'All I do is slave all day.'

Everything had to be just so,
she was forever on the go.
The house was always spick, and span,
but, she became an also ran.

Someone came next door to live,
who had so much more to give.
She was never over fussy,
nor was she a brazen hussy.

She had a smile for everyone,
life to her was full of fun.
Now hubby's gone to live next door,
he's found what he's been looking for.

So ladies please, do take care,
try to remember moaning Clair.
Housework you can always find,
Happiness is a state of mind.

M P Little

LEADING LIGHT

The old man trudged on, through the dirty grey snow,
      his energy gone, and his spirits so low.
He'd travelled far, and 'twas nearing night,
      but ahead in the gloom, he spotted a light.
His hope renew'd, and his stick called will,
      he attempted to walk up the slope of the hill.
He uttered a prayer, 'Please God let her be kind,'
      let this be a place, where a bed I can find.
The light from the window shone like a torch,
      as he made his way to the entrance porch.
He knocked with his gnarled old hand on the door,
      as he stood cold, and wet, and feet feeling sore.
A white hair'd lady answered his knock,
      and she turned the key to undo the lock.
She gasped 'You're cold, and wet to the skin,
      I've a fire in the lounge, please do come in.'
She brought towels, and clothing, put soup on to heat,
      and soon he felt warm from his head to his feet.
He thanked her most kindly, and asked if he may,
      sleep in her shed until it broke day.
You may sleep in the chair by the fire tonight,
      tomorrow we'll talk, and put wrong to right.
For deep in her heart she knew of his kin,
      it was her own father, she had taken in.

Lyn Brown

SCHIZOPHRENIA

There's something in my room
There's something lurking in the gloom,
I cannot see it
It follows me around
This demon from under the ground.

I hear voices whispering my name
I don't understand their aim,
Is it just my mind talking
Or a demon stalking.

Thoughts repeat like a beat
I am afraid to eat,
Someone's poisoned my food
That's what I conclude.

Drugs cannot help the ill
They just overdose and kill,
Anti-depressants do not solve
Because problems still revolve.

I am mad, I don't know why?
I have delusions I can fly,
Except really I am confused
As drugs I have misused.

Peter Walker

TELEVISION

Teaching, talking, travelling, telling.
Singing, sighing, shouting, selling.
Flickering images, people, places,
sounds and symbols, time and faces.

Worship, wailing, whispers, warring.
Bellowing, blasting, bewitching, boring.
Poignant pictures, startling scenes,
a shrunken perspective to fit the screen.

History, grief, national disaster,
memorable moments comedy and laughter.
No generation have witnessed such scenes
and wasted their lives in front of a screen.

J Jones

THOUGHTS AS THE DAY BEGINS

Isn't it lovely to wake in the morning?
I stretch out my legs, my toes are just twitching.
Mother calls loudly, 'Come quickly; your breakfast is ready.'
But I linger here; the hour is bewitching.
Mother shouts louder; 'Your breakfast is cold,'
'Get up at once; do as you are told.'
I put my feet on the floor; I nearly get back.
Mother gets angry; I don't need a smack.
So I do as I am told, like a dutiful daughter;
I dash to the bathroom and splash on some water;
I put on my clothes: I do up my hair:
If breakfast is cold, what do I care.
Mother hands me my coat; she does make a fuss.
'Hurry,' she says, 'you'll miss the bus.'
So I run down the road; How I wish I were free;
On a day such as this, there would be no schooling for me.
I would be off to the river; I would lie in the sun.
I would saunter back home when the day is quite done.
How I wish I were free; oh how I wish I were free;
On a day such as this, there would be no schooling for me.

E R Ebury

DOUBLOON

In the time it took for the lift
To travel up five floors,
In the gravity free space
Between the opening and closing of doors

You travelled beyond friendship
He smiled and stroked your hair;
He called you *Doubloon*
As you were standing in mid air.

28

He stroked your hair and said
It was reddish brown *like a hen,*
He watched you preen your feathers
And then he smiled again.

In the time it took for the lift
To travel to floor five,
He felt the electric thrill of your hair
And you never felt more alive.

Liz Loxley

HOLDING HANDS

It is not when I look at you
      That I feel old, nor when
I reach to touch my son's grave face
Nor envying my daughter's untamed grace,
      Nor catching in the mirror
A new wrinkle, more grey hair.

No, it is my hands - lying there
      Knarled like oak
I think of all the words they spoke
      To sad, young men
How they have prayed, pleaded
      Pressed against the door
Have stroked the softness of my children's heads

Have worked the yeast and flour
      Turned the beds
Have held - and failed to hold.
      In finger tips I have traced my love.
'I'd like to die like this,' he said
      As lying there in bed
We just held hands.

Megan Hostler

OLD FLAME

Do you mind if I come and see you next week?
Oh, by the way I'll be carrying a torch with me,
It's rather large I'm afraid,
You know like the Statue of Liberty's one?
The chances are it will probably
burn down the building
and everyone inside it too.
But there's absolutely no need for you to be concerned
I can guarantee you'll walk away unscathed
Experience has shown you're totally immune to my flames
So I know you won't mind about next week.

Sylvia Pollard

THE EMBRACE

When I lie at times, I see,
Visions of unbroken horsemen,
Half-lit, pictured galleries,
Friends of a friend of a stranger
Lost plastic bottles, drifting, almost seen,
The eyes of the one and all that's within them.
Streets, dim yet open
To all of the moon's fury and lies.
I see a thousand people, animals on lists,
But above all,
All I take, I lose, all I see,
The eyes of the one and all that's within them.

They haunt me still,
Days and nights crushed by their life.
The scene shifts; they remain,
Time and virtue weeping on my sorrow,
'Til their meaning fills me again.

30

Once more existence takes hold,
Her fingertip grip sweeps me away.
No sun burns my hidden extremes,
No tide lifts me above,
Until life is at last torn from my desperate hold,
She always will remain mine.
And when we embrace . . .

Paul Williams

PANIC ATTACK

Who am I? What is life? I am a child
Whose loving mother tucked me in, turned off
The light and left, so lately I hear her
Footfall on the stair. At once the blind
Primeval terror strikes: the dim room shrinks
And recedes, obscene paws claw at the drapes,
Tracing the familiar frightful pattern.
Downstairs, in earshot, sound of radio -
No help to me, nobody can know.
I speak my name: no meaning, no response.
Pinned down by the faceless beast, paralysed
And smothered, Angels waiting in the wings -
Now! Fling back the covers, to cheat and flee
The bed of death; wild of eye, with pounding heart,
To stand, seeking succour, at the window
And gaze out on the night.
In street lamp's shadow solid houses rear,
Out there, hung in unfathomable space,
The universe. The clock ticks, my heart calms -
Reluctantly my soul returns.
Ashamed, not understanding, I curl up
Wearily and bear my monstrous burden
In private: a child alone.

G Jones

THE COUNTRY CHURCH

It stands serene,
      cool and calm,
      steeped in silence
Yet loud with centuries of praise
Deserted, yet never alone,
      tranquil shadows,
      soothing darkness
Pierced by shafts of golden light,
Shining sun-enriched colours
      golden and glowing,
      muted, misty.
Pews polished by devotion
Mellowed by years of love
      waiting tirelessly
      for worship to begin.
Graceful columns stretch in mute appeal
To the hidden glories of Heaven;
Ancient walls contain the hopes of Man
Whilst richly gleaming wood is
      caressed by carving
      and flowers fall
      in careless cascade -
      immobile -
To delight the weary soul
It stands alone - yet never lonely -
Silent yet filled with song
Dead yet living - eternal.

L Slingsby-Tomlinson

BATH'S BRIGHT BOUQUET

The canal is still.
Narrow boats at peace
In the early morning.
Ducks sliding sweetly
Down dark water;
Heads tucked into sleep-swelled throats.
A moorhen clucks
In noisy adulation
Of her new-laid young.
A sudden surge
Of activity
Below the gleam
Blows rings expanding
Into stillness
As a fish
Aims high for breakfast.

The Abbey arches
Proud against the sky
As daylight
Paints its morning palette
Buttressed
By the gargoyles of the past.
While warmed
By mellow stone
And dreaming mullions,
The City's bright bouquet
Of florabunda
Joyously proclaims
The beauty of today.

Rhona Aitken

STAGBOROUGH SEASONS

Across a wintry landscape, beyond stark frozen fields,
Above the icy river you rise majestically.
And since time immemorial though seasons come and go
Along the years and decades like a guiding light you show.

Then spring's ethereal promise
Tints your trees with mists of green,
Until shy and softly shimmering
They blush with beauty from within.

That all may be renewed again
Each leaf, each blade of grass
Will shine again in springtime
All hardships are surpassed.

Next summer's awesome splendour
Swathes every dip and dale
With luxuriant deep-dappled foliage
Beneath skies cerulean.

Such richness, such abundance,
Does opulence make us complacent?
For in ignorance and greed we threaten you
There could never be a replacement.

To the breathtaking glow of autumn
When cascades of colour astound,
A dazzling performance of reds and golds
Nature's own finale grand!

And a century hence, will your trees still stand
Or will destruction be their plight?
Like the mists which hang in your valleys
All too easily swept from sight.

Gale Knight

SO MANY HURTS

Some through love some from pain
Some returning again and again
Some by tears that are hard to explain
Some by loss of Mum or Dad
Some by that baby you never had
Some by knife or gun
Some by a human tongue.
So many ways, we all try to understand
without God's helping hand
Once touching it you will live to know
all types of pains by asking him can go.

Dinah Goldstone

WHERE THE BLUEBELLS GROW

Across the fields we wander
My faithful dog and I
A true friend and companion
His love he does not hide
Down country lane abounding
His world not unlike mine
His tail forever wagging
The world to us sublime

Now into woods we wander
What beauty God hath made
With rustling leaves and song of birds
Serenity here reigns
Where cowslips, primrose, bluebells
And other flowers grow
God let us wander oft again
To where the bluebells grow.

Douglas Pearce

SHETLAND HOLDS ITS BREATH

Slap of the blackened waves
creep of the broken slick,
we hold our breath.
It is not too late. Lodged
on the rock it holds,
it keeps intact. Does it
hold intact?

Nothing bleeds
only the thick crude gush,
the arterial push of oil
through the vent.
It has broken and breaks.
Too late for tourniquets:
nothing stanches it now.

On the marred sand,
on the black slab, twenty
kinds of fish lie
belly up.

Marilyn Gunn

PLAYING TRICKS

Shadows
       but
can only
       I guess
be seen
       that's poetry
in a
       for you
certain light

Sara-Jane Arbury

STILL LIFE

What d'you say?
I thought I heard you mutter something
from those spiral stares that drill
from every hole around your head.

Yeah, what d'you say?
some words of whizz dumb emanate
from swollen lips and burning clumps
of momentary madness.

So you think you're chasing traces of imaginary places
that blow before you?
Well, you ain't seen nothing at all.

See you rise up from your resting place,
behind your bones -
your bed of roses glows
inside the sunset of your silence.

Watch you sit so proud,
and ride upon the mushroom clouds
around the walls that plague you,
strange whitewashed walls that still derange you.

And you think you're chasing traces of imaginary places
that just blow before you?
Well, you ain't seen nothing at all.

See the hole
so brightly bleached and stretching out before you;
like some prairie road
in all those films we saw together.

Fingers beckoning,
beguiling, ever closer,
ever further from the dreams
that hold you sucked inside your eyes.

K J Furber

ILLUSION

Harsh, burning lights,
Spinning, whirling,
Out of control.
Golden fantasy ponies
Frozen in time.
Moving,
Galloping endlessly
Yet never arriving.
Silver and gold,
Splashes of colour.
Blinding, glaring
In the light.
Spinning with the music,
uncontrollable.
Frenzied sounds and colours,
Challenging,
Fighting for supremacy.
Never succeeding,
Yet never giving in.
Fused together,
A timeless existence.
Two as one
Forever.

Until *Forever* ends.

The fantasy slows,
The magic disappears and
A beautiful lie is revealed.
Revealed as nothing more than
Illusion.

Arianne Weaver

TODAY'S NEWS

I pick up a daily tabloid newspaper
Confronted by a cover, dedicated to another scandal
Today, Di is to sue a photographer
Writes a 'close source,' from an entirely Royalist angle

The following page brings political speculation
A celebrity divorce and a special holiday offer
For the IRA and Sinn Fein - utter condemnation
And a small paragraph on the genocide in Rwanda

A teenage girl poses topless opposite a tax debate
For thousands of men; an early morning fantasy
Overleaf, a criminal who has decided to go straight
Editorial theories and a heart-warming love story

A page of advertisements and praise for the police
Letters to an agony aunt about sexual problems
An ill-disguised plea for terrorism to cease
A giant crossword and then, the classified sections

A photograph of a super-model in a revealing dress
Satirical cartoons and the astrological star signs
A pull-out guide to conquer executive stress
Finally, the racing form and the soccer stars of the time

I close the daily tabloid newspaper
Switch on the TV and listen to the day's news
I cannot understand how the versions differ
And then suddenly realise, I had merely bought an editor's views.

Steven J Smith

A WINTER'S SONNET

They're lucky, those whose love just slowly fades
In growing old; perhaps to friendship, worst
To passionless indifference as the Shades
Close in, inevitably, for the first.
The one who's left now selfishly lives on,
Unmoved, for death claims others every day;
Just fuelled by will because the mind has gone,
No thought or feeling left, nor urge to pray.
But then, our love: how to describe that sort?
Blazed forth in wartime, burning brightly yet,
Still warms our winter as the days grow short.
There's little, looking back, one could regret.
It concentrates the mind, this lurking fear,
Of loneliness for one of us, my dear.

G W Green

THE HONEY BEE

Of all the sweetest insects we
Would settle for the honey bee,
From dawn to dusk the workers toil,
Each one is to their Queen most loyal.

The workers, Ladies all first class
Provide the food for all - alas
The male or drone seeks only leisure
It seems his life is just for pleasure,

He's stupid fat and full of greed,
But yet the workers know they need
For preservation of the hive
To keep this monstrous drone alive.

The Queen is fertilised one day,
And then the workers have their say,
No longer will they feed the drones,
But bite and pinch them in their combs.

And once they're turned from out the hive,
They are unable to survive,
And once again our worker bee,
Provides us honey for our tea.

Stella Griffith

THE GARDEN

The first day of summer the last day of spring,
Everything has grown back again.
Some are dead and some are gone,
The old and decrepit replaced by the young.

Dead tress like skeletons provide a frame,
For the vigorous contenders of their once proud crown.
Enveloped by vine creeper and weed,
They can only look on the past and envy their seed.

Unattended the garden begins to explode,
No boundaries no more between once manicured lawns
                              and clean gravel paths.
Animals now have places to hide,
In deep lush grass and wildflower four feet high.

No-one noticed when the gardener died,
No-one asked where his body might lie.
But there in the grass amongst the old and the gnarled,
His body decays back to the past.

H Hammond

LONELY

Loneliness is when
I feel empty inside.
I feel as if nobody wants or needs me,
As if nobody would miss me
If I were gone.

I see best friends
Sharing secrets,
Having fun.
I swell up with jealousy.
Why can't it be me?
I wish. . . I wish. . .

I never seem to fit in with
Any of the games
My so called friends play.

The only best friend I could ever have
I have to imagine,
The only games I seem to fit in with
The ones I think of and play by myself.

Maybe I like playing on my own.
Maybe I like being left out.
Maybe it's good nobody cares.
Maybe I don't need a best friend.
Then again, maybe not!

Elizabeth Davey (11)

WHY CAN'T THEY UNDERSTAND

Why can't they understand
My body is whole
I have my arms,
My legs.
No sign can be seen of what is happening to me.
But, help me please.
Try to understand the pain I feel inside,
I'm in a turmoil
I can't escape.
I am trapped in the body of mine.
I'm in a feeling of despair
And hate.
A morass of depression I cannot define
Help me, tell me
What is happening to this world of mine.
Why do I hate it so being alone
Yes when I'm in company I want to go home.
I can't eat,
And my sleep is full of thoughts and dreams that I want to keep.
Bring back memories I loved so dear.
I could tell you about them
If only you had time to hear.
Please someone listen,
Please someone do.
I love the world,
My life
My home
I want to be more like you

Pat Ellwood

MY DAUGHTER MICHELLE

Of all the love that is in the world.
The greatest gift of all
Is the gift of love, I have for you
My darling little girl.

Janette Carol Hardy-Pierce

RIVER USK

I sit on a stone
With water slapping at my feet
Tall grass grows by me in clumps
Moss cushions my seat
I'm in the middle of the river
Which rushes around me. . .
In frustration and fury. . .
On its endless journey
Broken continuously by these stones. . .
Impeding its progress
So that it spits spray and spume. . .
Foam and fume. . .
Yet this display of temperament is superficial
No real intent of action
It's so shallow you see
Ideal for children playing with boats. . .
For crossing from side to side. . .
Stepping from stone to stone to reach fields
Fringed with kneeling trees
As if imploring the Usk to ease
Its hectic pace
Its daily race.

Pat James

POUND HILL - AVENING, 1995

No longer sheep nor shepherd dog
Disturb the peace of this quiet place,
Only intrusive motors clog
The narrow lane - fork tailed swifts race,
Loud mouse screaming, streaming, joining
Others in a mad swoop, trawling
Insects in the autumn evening,
Skimming nests tucked in stone walling.
From the sloping field opposite
A horse snort whinnies through damp nostrils,
Warm flanks its companion, owls tu-whit,
Tormenting wasps and flies are still.
In smoke grey sky sun sinks lower
Sets as a glowing fire - ember
Red spreads behind Holy Cross tower
Where the dead lie, clearly remembered,
Their resting place viewed from the hill.
The church, Matilda's attrition,
Conqueror William's spouse, responsible
Some say, for Brictric's death - a decision
On account he spurned her advances
As emissary of Edward to Baldwin
Count of Flanders, waiting her chance
Until she held the power of Queen -
Banished to Worcester from this sweet scene,
Where we enjoy 'Land of the Free'
With Gloucestershire folk of finest mien,
Most peaceful years of this century.
'though people search both far and near
They'll not find fairer view than here.

Rosemary Langdon

REFLECTION

At first I did not know her,
She was a stranger,
Just a woman staring out
From within the bevelled mirror,
For she was older than I'd thought
With lines across her face,
Weaving round their latticed threads
To form a patterned lace.
But as I watched she grew familiar,
As if I knew her years ago,
Before time had dimmed her once bright eyes
And flecked her hair with snow.

Long since she shared my childhood
Beneath an endless summer sky
When she filled my heart with hopeful dreams
That life would then deny,
Yet still I craved her company,
To have her at my side
And recollect the plans of youth
For which my spirit cried.
As I turned away she smiled,
Reviving dreams I thought had gone,
And I found that I was smiling too
For she and I were one.

Kit Moreton

SLEEP

Not dreams, the grand usher of monsters
Whom we stroke by day, but sleep
Whose footstep is soundless
Whose face is a stranger

46

Are you what we are when we are dead -
The edge of a world where all breath is held
In your numb hour do you unpick our seams?
Sleep, the eater of our counted sheep -
Their skins lie empty;
Shed like memories at the brains gate -
I am frightened for I cannot see you

When buried in your midnight, am I alone
In an echoless limbo, am I your only listener? -
Sleep, dark spinner of nothingness
You kiss my very bones

Sleep, are you what we are when we are dead?
Where time is exiled and consciousness fled
Do you spill out upon our pillows
From the cracks between the dream
When eclipsed by your silence
In the drugged arms of your oblivion.

Rebecca Henley

HOLIDAY HOME BY THE SEA

We have a little holiday home by the sea
It's only a caravan but it pleases me,
It's here at Redcliffe Bay,
It's lovely, we all do say,
Overlooking the sea,
No better place could we be,
We have so much fun,
Just lazing in the sun,
Down the lane is Walton Bay,
And that's another nice place to stay,
Yes we all agree,
We love our holiday home by the sea.

Mary Morris

TIGHT SKIRT

Once upon a time they thought,
That a woman could be bought,
Now in these enlightened days,
Men still take, but no-one pays.
Women's Lib - the freedom fight!
We still can't walk alone at night.
Equal rights? A source of mirth,
We can vote! For what it's worth.
We can't walk down the street alone,
And need a man to take us home,
We have no voice to just say 'no,'
And not the strength to turn and go,
And so they force their will again,
Leaving us with lasting pain,
They say of course, it's just fair do's -
You shouldn't wear those high-heeled shoes.
But did you know where you've just been,
You can still hear my lingering scream?

Rachel Kruft

SOMERSET SPELLS . . .

S   Starlit evenings
O   On the beach.
M   Moonlight kisses
E   Exchanged for keeps.
R   Romantic strolls;
S   Spell-bound dreams;
E   Enchantment holds
T   True love - so deep.

Rosemary A V Sygrave

GLORIOUS WESTON

Oh, I do love to be beside the seaside!
Especially Weston-super-Mare!
I love to sit on the sea front and breathe in the
        cool sea air.
I watch the donkeys giving rides to children with
        such tender loving care.
I love to walk the miles of sand
and take in the glorious views of surrounding land.
The wonderful white pier beckons me to play and have some fun.
Or when I am hot and bothered the open-air pool
        will surely cool me down.
If the sun stops shining and the rain clouds come
then I will find plenty of shops to wander round
in this pretty seaside town.

Anthea Youens

UNKNOWN WHIRLPOOL

When the moon glows
from the cloak of night,
the stars pray in silent slumber
out of the shadow of souls.
The earth's blood flows like
a dark river
sacrificed to secret joy

Beyond the whispers of time
unknown life breathes out
of the chasms of space,
where love and desire drown
in the universal whirlpool.

Julie Mears

BALLOON FIESTA

Suddenly they appear like bees serving their queen.
Time's a precious factor in this memorable event.
Hot air machines render forth the gift of life, as
busy bees untangle ropes and fasten willow baskets.
To experience man's determination to master flight.
They come from far and wide for this spectacular sight.

Like a mushroom spoor exploding with new life.
Time's a precious factor in this memorable event.
Crucial moments clash as people versus hot air power
take command.
To experience man's determination to master flight.
Oh! Ah! They cry, what a wonderful sight.

Man's determination rewarded the balloon ascends.
Time's a precious factor in this memorable event.
Local advertisements fill empty spaces.
To experience man's determination to master flight.
As the people search for recognition as their balloon
drifts out of sight.

The sky swallows greedily as they search for space in flight.
Time's a precious factor in this memorable event.
The feeding flame roars greedily to keep the balloon upright.
To experience man's determination to master flight.
The people follow hurrying to the place they land, for once again
they descend like mushrooms, the flame dies down and the
balloons are out of sight.

Mai Clarke

STRESS

I feel under stress
My life's in a mess
I'm all of a tiz
My heads in a whizz

I cannot stop frowning
I feel like I'm drowning
I'm starting to fret
And break into a sweat

I'm feeling uptight
And that isn't right
I'm tearing my hair
And longing to swear

My nerves, they are jangling
I feel I am dangling
Over a ledge
I'm right on the edge

I'm all of a panic
This is so manic
I'm dying to scream
Wake up from this dream

I'm getting an ulcer
Oh God! It's my pulser
Under this tension
I won't reach my pension

This must be a curse
It only gets worse
Everything's bad
Am I going mad?

      Aaaagh!

Jane Harris

CHANDOS STREET

Fish and chip papers abandoned
down salt and vinegar pavements,
wrapped around lampposts and
the old ladies ankles,
carrying her shopping basket full of cat food.
Stopping and talking under Maypole telegraph wires
to the children about the black cat
and the dancing dragonfly.
The old lady slowly walks up the street,
past the sweet shop,
two doors down from No 9 at half past eight and
three doors down from No 94 at nine o'clock.
Half an hour passes in the street
looking down the terraced row at
row after row of gardens growing
flowers and nettles, full of pride and neglect.
Clay chimney pots bake in the sun,
          without fires
on ocean going roof tops, amongst
the armada sail of TV aerials, and
a black wing pirate watches above
the starling eves.
Strangers in passing take curious glances
through front parlour windows
at piano rooms, aspidistras, Victorian
on marbled fireplaces, with lampshade
bookshelves in cosy corners.
The traffic moves up and down the street
at irregular intervals, familiar street cars,
some with warm bonnets for cats

Come and go from territorial parking spaces
in front of red polished door steps
and porches occupied with tropical plants,
pram wheels, hats and walking sticks.
By the time the yellow bus stopped
and moved away at the end of the street
the old lady was gone.

Arfon Williams

BRANDON HILL, BRISTOL

I live by the hill. It is dying.
The grass is burnt and
Nobody wants to sit down there
Anymore, because the grass is so
Hard it hurts.
And the trees are crying
Out for water. Their
Bony roots feeling ever deeper, like
Clawing fingers.
And ants wrestle one
Another for the food that
Isn't there.
And the sun is merciless.
And the sky, blue as an ocean, releases
No water.

Yet, I remember Spring, when it rained so
Hard that the hill wept
Streams long after the
Rain had stopped.

And the rain has stopped.
And the hill is dying.

Yet, still I can see a grandmother
Raping the blackberry bushes. . .

Claire Williamson

MY CHILDREN

In the passing of a year
I watch my children grow,
Become people.
Last week they crawled,
Yesterday they spoke their first words
Today they left school,
Tomorrow they will leave home.
My life took years,
And in the carrying of them
I aged decades.
And in the blinking of my eyes
I missed and lost out
On this delight.

In the passing of a year
The leaves have changed
Their green for gold.
They became
In front of me
Houses and roads.
And I did nothing
Stood dumb
And aged quietly
Valleys of centuries
Wiped out in seconds.
I watched only my children
And lost my planet.

S Coombes

54

ANOTHER MEANS OF DYING

The sword that had hung menacingly over his head,
Fell with alarming swiftness,
In an instance he died.
Yet he lived,
He knew he lived he could feel the pain,
He could feel,
The cold,
Slowly it rose first his toes,
The ankle now the knees
Cold so cold,
So this was death,
But he lived
The coldness crawled into his gut!
He gritted his teeth,
To cry out would bring shame,
I am . . . a man!
Once but no longer,
He was dead.

The coldness engulfed him
The man died,
His dreams his ambition his being,
All dead.

He breathed but he was dead,
No,
Worse,
He was redundant.

A L Perrett

MY TRENDY, OBTUSE, ELITIST POEM

Satsumas, bloomers, rings in a row.
Pedals, medals, lumps of white dough.
Dogs, frogs, things in the dark.
Eagles, beagles, song of a lark.

Crates, mates, six foot tape measure.
Filth, tilth, things you can treasure.
Plates, gates, hedges of privet.
Mustard, custard, shiny new rivet.

Ships, slips, wild geese in flight.
Cars, stars, wind in the night.
Stop me, bop me, it's got out of hand.
Why this I this, I don't understand.

Tendentious? Pretentious! A whole lot of muck.
Arty farty, the writer's a schmuck.

Peter McDonagh

FASTEST RIVER IN THE WEST

Fastest river in the west
Fastest river in the land
Snatching the young child at its breast
Swallowing the dog into its whirlpool hand.
You deceive us with your beauty.
But, lest we forget
You demand our respect
The child, the dog you forget
As you rush down to join the channel
You will not care as we do who you take all the way
Fastest river in the west must get to Bristol today.

Heather Burvill

JAGGED EDGE

The glass of the window is shattered,
The weather has rotted the frame,
Born with genetic inheritance -
It is living that's leaving the stain.

Intimidation, injustice and cruelty,
Thoughtlessness, selfishness, pride,
Ignorance, rejection and hatred
Invisible walls that divide.

An increase in wealth verses poverty,
Humanity walks the trapeze,
Ignoring the gross inequality
Our actions promoting disease

On course for a mindless existence
Society control
Humanity dying of freedom
No boundaries, no justice, no goal.

Helen Jones

DICK TURPIN

In 18th century England, far away and long ago.
There was but a young butcher, whose life would end with woe.
From a humble butcher to a legend he became.
He became the famous highwayman, Dick Turpin was his name.
He had a pretty horse. It's name it was Black Bess.
And every time he rode her, the people liked him less.
He got in with old Gregory's Gang and then with old Bob
King.
A hanging at The Mount in York is what this life did bring.

Juliet Pyke

PRIVATE LIVES OF HUSBAND AND WIFE

Husband: Evening dear, now where's my tea?
                          I've had a hard day at the office you see
                          The monthly sales and figures are down
                          And secretary's typing makes me frown.

                          I'm glad the kids are up in bed
                          Their noisy clatter goes straight to my head
                          Well, as nothing's going on round here
                          I think I'll go and drown in beer.

Wife: Listen to me, I'm lonely you see
                          I'm stuck in this house when I long to be free
                          I've watched TV, washed nappies all day
                          Are you surprised I've nothing left to say?

                          Happiness, is it such a sin?
                          I find it unattainable within
                          There's nothing more left to be said
                          I think I'll go and cry in bed.

Pamela James

KING OF ALL I CAN SEE

Riding along on the top of the bus,
What wonderful things to see.
There's Mrs Brown in the baker's shop
Buying cakes for afternoon tea.

The fishmonger's cat is on the shed roof,
Stretching out to soak up the sun.
The McGregor twins are off to the park
To play and have lots of fun.

Into the shops in each busy street
The people rush to and fro.
But once in a while, they'll stop with a smile
To speak to someone they know.

Apples and oranges, cabbage and peas
Are all displayed in the street.
If they're knocked, they fall to the floor
And get squashed beneath everyone's feet.

In the centre of town, a mile away
Stands the clock tower, straight and tall:
When I'm riding along on the top of the bus
I pretend that I'm king of it all.

Joyce Hopkins

IN A PERFECT WORLD

In a perfect world
I'd be made of money
I'd not get drunk
I'd not be moody.

In a perfect world
The sun would shine
We'd go round smiling
Though we didn't need to.

In a perfect world
I'd be younger
Have more hair
Regain my figure.

In a perfect world
We'd call a truce
Enjoy the time we have
Make the most of life.

In a perfect world
I wouldn't write this poem!

J R Lovering

LES REGRETS

When I was just a young girl,
Had senses all awhirl,
My long, lean, leathered lover
Loved her Harley more than me.

And so,
Sod off, I said,

And then,
She did.

And now,
She's dead.

And me?
I live at home,
With mother.

E Woodsford

ESCAPE ROUTE

In a foetus position like a child
Hiding in the bathroom because he's wild
The hatred exploding from his mouth is sad
It hits at my centre and driving me mad

A broken heart like shattered glass
A rabbit trying to bury itself in grass
If I could find a comfortable burrow
There'd be no worrying about tomorrow

How can I escape him he must be ill
Perhaps an injection or maybe a pill
My identity gone, don't know who I am
Days are gone to be skipping like a lamb

Please someone give me strength and pride
There's nothing wrong with me, I shouldn't hide
I'm beautiful, fun and full of love
If only I could fly like a little dove

A magic carpet is what I need
I'll wish real hard that should do the deed
Look down on him as I fly through the air
He can't reach me now, and I don't care

Olive Weller

MY DAUGHTER

Daughters come and daughters go,
My daughter is the best I know
She brings me joy, she brings me pain
But I'll never know her like that again!

She's beautiful but oh so sad
And disillusioned with all that's bad!
I try to help, it's not enough
She needs to be of sterner stuff.

This life is tough, you have to cope
No good living just in hope
The world will change, she says and soon
I say yes and I can fly in a balloon.

Her faith in God is really strong
So I pray please help her along
Let your love upon her shine
But leave alone the girl that's mine

For part of me she'll always be
I've nurtured her from twig to tree
My love for her is oceans deep
Until and beyond that final sleep!

Joy Toms

THE DAY THAT I DREAM

The sun was so bright, with you
At my side and no-one around.
Since I fell for you, I'm still in
Love with you.
You are the sunshine of my life.
I look into your eyes thru' the
Pouring rain, feel the rhythm
Of my heart.
When I'm feeling blue, I wanna get
Lost in your lovin' soul.
Tonight will be long, the night will
Be cold. There's a treasure in my
Heart of love lasting gold.
Hold me close, hold me tight,
In the arms of love your shelter
From the cold.

C Hornby

THE UNTAMEABLE ONES

They hop and flop
When walking along
I can hardly contain them.
When getting dressed
I have to stuff them in my bra
Or they would slide away then.

When I watch the telly
They slip onto my belly
The nipples can be seen
Pointing to the screen

No matter how I kneed them
To make them disappear
They only seem to grow again
To my great despair.

62

Please let me have some little ones
And take away my tyre
So I look nice and slim again
And once more be admired.

Gisela Cooper

THE STARVING CHILD

The little wizened face looked up at me,
Drawn and grey, and full of ancient wisdom,
Small claw-like hands
That clasped a swollen body,
Dry lips that whispered '*bread*,'
The sad child eyes, dim, filled with pain
Had seen so many dead.

My heart is drained of pity,
Where can I seek release for them?
The dead all speak,
A million childish voices -
'We had no chance to live,
The cards were stacked against us
We had no hostages to give
To famine.'

Can we do nothing - nothing
But watch them crumple,
Fall and lie,
Die starving in the gutters,
While all around the hungry
With empty anguished faces
All unheeding
Pass them by?

Alex Turner

HAPPY HOUR

Chalk, on the wall -
'A spirit free with every beer!'
Free spirits would be strangers here.
In chains of alcohol

we tag along
by one and one - no company,
alone in our society -
a melancholy throng.

And start upon
a deathly race to satiate
the devil we adored, and hate,
and call Oblivion.

So little heed
we take, as we infest the bar,
of who we were, and what we are,
in thrall to what we need.

We know the rules.
The hour elapsed - the welcome ends.
Our sorry presence here offends
the transitory fools

who bray and sneer
in ready moneyed gaiety,
with neither wit nor will to see
their future, acted here.

Dave McClure

THE LONELY SOLDIER

Lonely soldier,
        Do you dream of days gone by, and reminisce
of wartime songs,
And coming home to smiling faces, and a kiss.
        Did you return to happy days.
Or does your mind, instead of safe return
Remember dead, and suffering,
        and wicked ways.
Did you read of news from home
        When on your wartime bed you lay.
Or was it always news you heard.
From other soldiers loved ones far away.
        When the mighty war was won
Did you have a tale to tell,
        Or did you end it just as you begun,
Back inside the lining of your shell.
        Perhaps another lonely soul you found
Somewhere there, along the path of life.
        Maybe he fought and died on foreign ground.
Perhaps he was the only friend around.
Do you think of him when trumpets sound
        Then does the silence cut you - like a knife
When an old man looks into the night.
        If the only thoughts he can recall
Are painful loneliness, and tears of fright,
        Do we really have the right
To shine a victory light.
        Did we ever win the war at all?

Christine Banner

THE BEAST OF THE MOOR

He wove his weary way through the trees,
The dark, dank, dripping trees.
The moss was dense underfoot,
And the air was cool and wet, and he was
Tired, oh so very tired.
Then abruptly he was out, out in the
Glistening, gleaming, glittering sunlight.
Beyond him stretched the purple moor,
With crags and crannies, and high heaps of stones,
Smooth, slippery, solid stones.
He stood motionless for an instant, then set off,
His nostrils inhaling the fresh morning air,
His ears catching the gurgling of a bubbling stream.
Then all at once he heard a different sound,
A snickering, snarling, sneering sound,
And there on the shoulder of a boulder,
Was a cruel black beast,
With rangy body, and dark shining fur,
And as he halted, it sprang,
Crashing down from on high onto him,
Roaring, ripping, rupturing.
It tore through his flesh, and a scream filled his head,
And then darkness again,
Dark,
Dank,
Dripping,
Darkness.

Weeks later, the Farmer, searching for a sheep,
Stumbled across the carcass,
He scratched his head,
And said,
'Another Fox dead!'

S E Fernandes

POPPIES

See how the poppies grow.
All in a single row.
Each one has a story to tell of the soldiers' who fell.
They won't grow old as we do.
For fathers and mothers, sweethearts, time has stood still.
Because the shock of war was to kill.
As the sun goes down, dawn sweeps across the field,
One can almost see their flaxen faces.
You can hear the grass murmuring in the breeze.
The soldiers were so weary they laid their heads to rest.
The Lord only takes the best.

The tears from a mother's eyes was like blood from a wound, flowing
fast and warm upon her cheek.
When the sun goes down and night time falls.
We shall remember them our boys.
No more listening for that key in the door to see your loved ones
Once more.
Your heart beating fast, full of love and joy, what was once your
little boy,
You fear the war will destroy.
With a cheeky smile on his face you hear a soft voice whisper
'Mum, I'm going to war,'
I run to him to embrace, with the screams of horror raging through
my mind.
My son is going to war, proudly wearing his uniform, with one
thing in mind.
Fighting for his country and mankind.

Marie Graham

BLACKBERRY PICKING

The conflicting people inside of me
Identify with the angry buzzing of bees
The powerful sun radiates the heat of ice
In comparison to the rage in my heart.

Eager chubby hands reaching, grasping
Ripping the soul, the fruit, from the bush
Too much pressure and sticky blood does emerge -
This is my father's frame I destroy.

The revenge is sweet, my taste buds liken to it
But the nourishment is never enough
Unfulfilling; I still feel empty
Food cannot compensate for the fullness of love

Jessica M Price

THE FIRST WINTER OF WIDOWHOOD

The last migrant bird has left the autumn sky,
Leaving a dull monotony of unbroken endless grey.
Tired trees delay the urge to fade and fall asleep.
In a final defiant dance of riotous colour,
That I have no desire to see.

Human contact lessens with the shortening days.
Doors are firmly closed against the coming night.
Windows curtained over, keeping comfort safe within.
Outside I stand in solitude, in cold and rain and dark,
Conscious of my misery, oblivious of stars.

The home I knew and loved, is home for me no more.
The dear sweet taste of memory lies bitter on my tongue.
Company alone, is in a voice my ears imagine.
And hands that stretch for warmth towards an unshared fire,
Find little solace in the bleak of winter.

M Bloomfield

DESPAIR

Today I felt crushed
By the weight of your tears
As you cried for the first time
of your pain and your fears
My strength deserted me
In the face of your grief
      Stolen away
      Sadness the thief
      Helpless, I held you,
      What could I say,
To give you the strength
to face a new day?
Clichés came easily
No help at all
Could you not hear, God,
The despair in my call?

Mary Cassidy

I KNOW 'COS I'VE BEEN THERE

The darkest depths of guilt.
The garage of despair.
The school of disappointment
The team of defeat.
The interview of embarrassment.
The team selection of humiliation
The dream of failure.
The oblivion of alcohol.

The bright star of birth
The bedroom of elation.
The pinnacle of life.
The cathedral of hope.
The glorious palace of love.

John Griffiths

SO DIFFERENT

Beneath the railway arch at the crack of the Day,
and you're waiting there after the rain,
and the rain beneath your feet has been cleaning these streets
as if it was washing all the dirtiness away,
and the chimneys are distant and grey
like the memories that you're allowing to fade
what you are now and what you wanted back then
are so different. . .

In the cold morning breeze you are starting to freeze
and the token sunshine does nothing to please,
and with a push and a shove your lift's picking you up
to ferry you off to distant factories
where last night seems so far away
and your dream girl was looking your way,
and what you had planned to say and what you eventually said
were so different. . .

And when, at last, you get home, from the taxi you're thrown
on the pavement you land with their last cheerios,
it could have been different, well, that's just how it goes
when you choose a job that pays just enough money for clothes,
and your ambitions seem so far away
because you decided to let them decay
but your life is filled with few complications,
it's so different. . .

Beneath the railway arch at the end of the day,
the rain has washed all your high hopes away
and the people whose lives involve pressure and lies
wish they could be more like you as from their windows they spy,
because their ambitions lead them all of the way
and in the end, they were hopelessly astray,
and all they want to do is lead life like you do,
that's so different.

Jason Till

70

WHITE HORSE

Hand in firm hand, with swinging gait,
Over downland spring and tuft we pass
Through harebells, skylark and fussing sheep.
The skyline, gladdening our warming hearts
Waves and whispers in the zephyr breeze,
As yellowed wheat and speckled grass
Roll glistening in the silent heat.

Then, way up on the hill, we found
This once proud home of Iron Age fame,
Where, ancient kings of a wide domain
Guarded cladded hills and lynchet plain.
Faint echoes; the cries of bloody war;
As bold warriors, fair and azure-eyed,
Seized this green land for evermore

Silent images now at rest,
His all seeing, unblinking eye,
From ridge to chalky ridge, surveying,
Hides vain sacrifice, heartache, pain,
As, long tail flowing, fair mane blowing,
Ghostly, silently, he gallops by
Cross the green and rolling winds of change.

Now, sun alone shines bloody red
Praising forgotten heroes dead.
Treasuring warmly our stolen peace,
Ignorant of these myriad times,
Over downland spring and tufted grass
Hand in firm hand with swinging gait
We, mere humble trespassers, pass.

Jane Le Bon

GEORGETTE

Georgette's the desire of every man's heart,
Thought she's nothing to look at and a bit of a tart.
Yet whenever she smiles and gives men the eye
They are eager to please her and would happily die
For a touch of her rough hands or a kiss from her lips
Or a stroke of her rather voluminous hips.

But Georgette is fickle; she blows hot and cold.
She's happy to handle, but never to hold.
Men think they have won her and found their Miss Right,
But they're out on the pavement the following night.
While she's down at the disco with her latest man,
Who thinks he can own her as no-one else can.
His arms close around her as they take to the floor,
And she winks at the bouncer who stands at the door.

Laura Hill

A DAY'S END

The sky was the shade of wet Delabole slate.
The sea was a similar blue.
That nine fifteen June evening seemed very late;
not even a seagull flew,
when down from the cloud, like a dropped dinner plate,
the Sun slithered into view.

A ribbon of pewter between sea and sky
arrested Her flat, listless sphere,
but slowly, so slowly, She slipped, with a sigh,
to rest on the sea like a tear.
And then the Sun sank, as the wind gave a cry,
She drowned in an ocean of fear.

Caroline Burchell

FORGIVENESS

Sub-patterns
Weaved
Into relationships.
Vines of sometime
Misunderstanding
Hurt
Anger
Threaded within
The past -

Scars are trenches
Where survivors hide.
Your words of irritated rage
Like
Bullets.

I'm sorry,
You say, I was angry this morning
And taking it out on you -
It doesn't matter, I say -
My soldiers crouching for
Survival in the scars -
I'm not bothered, I say,
(Make the coffee,
. . . but I'm shaking)
It's just sub patterns
Weaved
Into relationships.

Michelle Blower

HOLLOW

You're on your own, head held low, fallen from grace
You picked the bone and you were wrong now you must face
The hollow music that you wrote because you feared
The worst would happen believing everything you heard
It's ringing loud but you can't turn it down.

The words are flying, 'what possessed me to say that
I could have exorcised my anger, now I don't even have that'
You drew the blade before you realised it was cold
Thrust it so deep and now you'll turn it on yourself.

Losing blood fast, you're cutting out your heart
Tearing your heart to find the blackened part
Losing blood fast catch the black stuff in a jar
And paint a picture of your past.

The hollow music will not stop until the time
Every black drop of blood has fallen in the jar
And you have filled in every space that you can find
The picture's dried and jealous blood is all you see

But look again, you can't believe your eyes
Believe your heart, it's all healed up inside
And on the screen you see a figure form
A little beard, a pitchfork and a pair of horns

Holding his hands over his ears and screaming now
It's ringing loud the hollow music sounds
It's ringing loud but he can't turn it down.

William Rees

74

UNTITLED

Out of the lavender bush one summer day
Four baby hedgehogs crawled around
What joy to see the little dears
Looking for insects on the ground.
They had lost their mother so to fill their need
We put out meat and fat for them to feed
Then back to the lavender bush to rest
What a sweet smelling home to make a nest.

Mary Garrett

ABORT

Water's edge, waves lapping
pulling the silence back
from the fires that burn
in her blood.

Does she know what lies there?
How does she feel
as countless blades
drive through her.

Mooning walls, sighs of above
her eyes reflect pools of
her mind,
dank and destitute she wonders.

Images waver in the reflection
calling out.
Escape the lines of her thought
undo the haunting.

V Turner

LOVE IS

Must you brush my face
With your lips as we dance,
This last dance that we shall dance?
Don't you know,
Your fingers in my hair
Are as claws that rip
My unprotected heart.

But love is no dance,
Choreographed and neat,
Love is bitter,
Not sugary sweet,
Love is no summer meadow,
Free from rain,
Love is mulled heartache
Laced with pain

I thought that love
Was a game of share alike,
But how wrong I was,
My errors are so plain now,
You've shown me that because,

Love is a wave without a beach,
Always reaching for something,
But just out of reach,
Love is a fawn without his flute,
Frustrated and bitter,
Deaf dumb and mute,

So what do I care,
Just torture me more,
Rip my heart up,
With your hands of claws.

Mark Foster

A BABY BOY

With your first cry
I wept for joy
For I was so proud
Of my baby boy

You took your time
To come into my life
Now I feel complete
A mother and a wife

With each day
You bring more joy
I'll love you forever
My baby boy.

Penny Trevett

ESCAPE

A lady in pain, more than a heart can bear
A dagger delivered, plunged into unknown fear!
The man she loved, could love no more
Soon the final closing door.
Twenty years had melted away
In one unsuspected Saturday
In a heart something had died
A body shook as the last tears were cried
Thrown into a life of utter loneliness
The pain found impossible to suppress!
In her hand the residue of overdose
In her head the lost memories and repose
A fleeting replay of a life - now done
A love whose course had prematurely run
An instant stocktake of the final sum
Life's breath gone. . . and the pain overcome.

Joe Watt

OF MICE AND DOGS

Bertie and Gertie were two little mice
Who spent most of their time eating cheeses and rice
They never had washes not yet combed their hair
And when they weren't eating, slept in an armchair.

Now an old dog called Rusty liked that same armchair
He spent hot summer days and wet evenings there
His coat was all shaggy and snugly warm
And the mice were most grateful in their little dorm.

All would have been well if they'd kept it that way
But two can live cheaply as one, so they say,
And soon that old armchair was swarming alive
Those two little mice now turned into five.

Poor rusty was peeved by this state of affairs
And suddenly thought of the spare bed upstairs
He ambled away, hoping no-one would see
'For I don't want them mice a'following me.'

He stretched out full length and gave a big sigh
Then jumped off the bed with a terrible cry
For hanging on to his coat and each one was there
Twice fifty damn mice from that old armchair.

The moral of this story can plainly be seen
Always be sure that you know where you've been
Uncertain friends, leave behind, when you've gone
Or they'll stick just like glue and you've got hangers on.

Irene Benjamin

THE WHISPERING GIANT

Concorde Oh Bird of Silver Grey,
How I'd love you to fly me far, far away.
Over mountains and plains,
To cities of my dreams.
You and I would be like a King and Queen,
Flying over out kingdoms of dreams.
Reaching from shore to shore,
What a wonderful experience,
Who could ask for more.

They write songs about ships and other planes,
But never has anyone had such brains,
To write a song about this beautiful plane.
There we have it at our finger tips,
So why not find a song a tribute that would fit,
This majestic whispering giant,
With wings that span the world.

Oh! How I wish I could fit a tune,
To these heartfelt words,
Off all the rubbish that's churned out on radio and TV.
They seem to write such ridiculous words,
Of space and wars and suffering
When right in front of all our eyes,
Is the very thing we should all be proud of.
And boy! How we could sing.

So come on all you song writers, where's your imagination,
If I am an ordinary middle-aged housewife,
And I can say the words,
To praise these clever men
In this our generation
For giving us this beautiful *Concorde*
Let's see some inspiration
A song to sing, for the *Whispering Giant* give it to the nation.

Dotties Ditties

DAD'S BIRTHDAY

Another birthday has come around
To your wife and children your love has
                                    been sound,
With that in mind I wish to say,
I hope you have a wonderful day.

You're sometimes happy, sometimes mad,
But, we'll always respect you, because
                                    you're our dad,
From you we are able to get advice,
Knowing you're there for us, that's nice.

So, I've written this poem just for you,
A splendid dad and grandad too,
We treasure the moments more and more,
We spend as a family, that is for sure.

So once again, from your daughter and son,
This birthday wish is surely the one,
To show you how much we appreciate,
As dads come, you really are great.

A Gibbs

THE SEARCH

I've stood alone upon that rocky cliff gazing out to sea.
The wind so strong against my face the breath is taken from my lips.

I've stood alone amongst the Autumn trees on a bright but frosty morn.
The frozen leaves all around, a blanket for the winter days ahead.

I've stood alone at the Hotel window looking down on the scene below.
Away from home those streets are full with people I'll never get to know.

I've stood alone waiting for that silence, wanting for that peace.
But the constant tick of the mantle clock denies me such a treat.

I've stood alone and wondered why? I look so deep yet never find.
So many thoughts, so many fears, just where to go from here.

I've stood alone to search for answers, to contemplate the great unknown.
Stood alone? I know, so this is for you, to show you're not just on your own.

Phil Bateman

THE MONTY

Still waters run not deep between the banks
Except within the locks.
The rattle of the paddle gear
Disturbs the silent evening air.
A narrowboat glides gently to the bank.
Oh! Please not there
Where
Beneath the coppiced trees, the careless rank
Of orchids rise from faded primrose clumps
Where snowdrops grew.
The crew
Dismount and light the barbecue.
No cars, no trains,
No aeroplanes
Just the gentle strains
Of blackbirds evensong
The gentle plop of rising fish
The rustle in the reeds of shrews
And dragonflies
With swooping flight
Look out upon this country scene
The ripening corn amid the green
The lonely curlew cries
Good night, sleep tight
See you at dawn's early light.

John Cotterill

SNOW IN MAY

The flowers were blooming
The sun was shining to the tip of his tongue
Suddenly it stopped.
Snow began to fall
Everybody ran inside
And the next day snow covered everywhere
Even the tops of houses!
But one little girl went out to play,
Called all her playmates out
They all started to throw snowballs at each other.
And the little girl said why don't we make a snowman.
They asked their mums could they go sledging.
And the next day all the snow had gone.
And they were very, very sad.
But the little girl had had her birthday
wish for snow in May.

Phillippa Bengry

THE TREE

The tree stands all alone,
In rain sun and winter snow.
An air of magic with a mysterious shroud,
Trying to touch the very clouds.

It cannot see hear or touch,
But can sometimes inspire with a single look.
It's home to birds, squirrels and alike,
Keeping them safe within its sight.

It's been there for over one hundred years,
The silent witness to all our fears.
If it could speak a tale it would tell,
Of our ancestors who knew it well.

N B Miller

AND SO TO SHED

Gone is the sleeper cabin where I sat
To make my ticket out when cold winds blew.
Healed are the scars where once the hot ash spat
And spluttered as we cleaned the firebox through.

I lay my weary arm upon the stile
Which once I could vault lightly over.
My leaden legs I need to rest awhile,
It's years since I was such a rover. . .

. . . My eyelids droop, once more the platform rings
With hobnailed boots, young men with heavy packs
To these quiet parts a laden troop-train brings,
Fighters with freedom resting on their backs.

Bright posters warn us, 'Careless talk costs lives'
In paint-starved waiting rooms, and *Walls have ears.*
Shabby and dark the last down train arrives,
And so to shed, stumbling through blacked-out years.

At last the war is won, the railway *ours,*
But all too soon there comes the danger sign.
Upon the small branch lines the Boardroom glowers.
The axe hangs poised above the Fairford line,

And fall it does in spite of all our fight
To save our trains, our jobs, our railway trade.
We spoke of service but here might was right;
No hope. *Uneconomical,* they said.

Unchecked the fireweed blazes, brambles twine.
Like whistle-blasts their cries, the black swifts dart
And wheel and swoop above the Fairford line,
A requiem for a driver's broken heart.

K B Law

A REASON

My husband is a football fan,
I dread the football season.
You wonder why I should moan,
but I have got a reason.
Before we were married,
he'd take me to the odd game.
But now the rings on my finger,
Things are not the same.
He likes to go with the boys
and be a typical lad,
leaving me at home,
feeling really mad.
If he would take me to,
A couple of games this season,
Then I would not moan at him,
Cause I wouldn't have a reason.

Tracy Weaver

RETROSPECT

Teddy bear in the chair,
Sometimes I'm sad to see you there -
For long ago
My little son so cherished you.
       But now
Those days are gone.

The memories live on
And in my heart
My children always play a part
Of years gone by -
And still I yearn
To feel those childish hands
Upon my face.

Dear God give grace
That with thy love
I do not weep for distant days
But give thee praise
For joys that I have known.

Marcella Pellow

LOVE'S EPITAPH

Where you have clipped the wings of my soul,
Emotions flutter against the cage of my heart,
And I know I shall soon die.

Where once my hopes flowed free,
Soaring high in expectation,
I only see you and the prison of my fears.

I am damned by love.

Where once I existed,
I can not longer see who I am.

I am fettered to the being mirrored in your eyes.
I have lost definition.
I am prostitute.
I am you.

There are demons plucking at the flesh of my mind.
Vulture-in on my decay.

Soon I will no longer exist.

In wanting you.
I am dead.

A J Foster

SEVERN FLOODS

I have seen
Those green and gorgeous days
Each one - a year,
When bluebelled wells were sweet and clear,
And trees clawed skies, until their branches broke,

Then, flooded rivers spoke of somewhere
far upstream,
Banks I'd never seen, whispered, winked,
To an always cocked
And now mocked, ear, I think!

I listened then to willows bent in spate
Bringing news from - God knows where,
Tide marks and the currents race were headlines
With days old dates,
Inscribed with muddy print.

Today, I see the news,
Watch pictures aerial views,
And, question dreams of floods,
I can't remember now how a willow bends,
To scoop at floating death, and bursting promises.

But still they come from God knows where,
the floods, and spells evaporate in air
for doubting Thomas's,
Whose only waters now, are tears,
Which merely kiss neglected garden mint

John Thomas

86

TORTURE

Torture why do it,
what's the need,
inflicting pain,
on a different creed

Torture why do it,
hurting others,
giving pain,
to our sisters and brothers.

People chained up,
losing their strength,
forgetting outside,
and what it meant.

Forgetting their lives,
they used to lead,
they want you to stop,
they beg and plead.

The blood the cuts,
the darkened rooms,
the people as if,
there in their tombs.

Their life is over,
or that's what they feel,
so write a letter,
this is an appeal.

Ema Eykyn (15)

CHANGING TIMES

Have you noticed how print's getting smaller
It can't possibly be failing sight
I shouldn't *need* glasses at my age
But I still see my future as bright.

Have you noticed how stairs are made steeper
I can't *think* why they build in more height
Yet *that's* why they're now far more tiring
But I still see my future as bright.

Have you noticed how doctors are younger
Such youthfulness doesn't seem right
Years ago, there were only mature ones
But I still see my future as bright.

Have you noticed how youngsters behave now
Not like us, who were fine and upright
We behaved with impeccable virtue
But I still see my future as bright.

Have you noticed how people now mumble
It doesn't seem very polite
It's becoming an effort to hear them
But I still see my future as bright.

Have you noticed how pleasures are changing
Now, the simple things give more delight
It takes years to learn how to *enjoy* life
So I *know* that my future is bright!

B J Fowler

LEARNER

I'm a learner driver.
Lessons I've had a score,
Going out driving is,
Like going out to war.
I'm getting quite a driver,
My technique is unique,
I never give way to pedestrians
That try to cross the street.
Halt signs and white lines
Were made for men of leisure,
Left signs, right signs,
Not put there for pleasure.
Junctions and cross roads.
Roundabouts and lights,
Traffic Laws and Highway Codes,
Were not made for me.
So if a lady driver, you should ever see,
Not a moment tarry
Away from her *flee.*

Irene Shaw

FRITILLARY

Yes,
Pretty one,
Butterflies are like flowers.
They flitter - flutter through the day,
Just like you,
You dancing flower,
You singing butterfly!

Alan Turley

FIVE FURLONG START, BATH

Blue dome above
Rolling downs green
Oolite stone walls
Encompass the scene.
      One, two, three, four
      Contrails on high
      Fraying white lines
      Traversing the sky.
One or two swifts
Dart in the breeze
Twist and drop down
Over wind sloped trees
      Five furlongs away
      See the ship ride -
      The stands, to receive
      First wave of the tide.
Jockeys aboard
Canter to post
Enstalled, they burst
Like a devil host.
      Distant crowds roar
      And commentary staff
      Calmly announce
      Photograph.
What odds the winner?
I've had a good run
For my money
Here in the sun.

John Rumming

THE LEGEND OF THE HOT BATH

The story begins many years ago,
There were many cures that we didn't know,
Then a legend was made by an early king,
Who discovered a cure, in a spring.

King Bladud lived a solitary life,
When leprosy struck him like a knife,
Then he discovered by chance one day,
That there really and truly was a way,
A way to be cured and it suddenly twigged,
He had to roll in the mud with his pigs,
So he rolled in the mud - what a strange thing,
But the secret was really in the spring,

The king went out to tell of his cure,
Others got better, you can be sure,
Thousands came to use these springs,
More were cured - what a wonderful thing!

Hannah Brunt (14)

LOST LOVE

I would have made a willow cabin at his gate
I could have travelled in the realms of gold
A masterpiece of artistry create
From memories of love in days of old.

I wanted him to fly me to the moon
And sing me love songs with an old guitar
But all we had was just a month in June
I touched the sky but never caught a star.

Mavis Winter

DRIVEN

Mentally, I'm always doing it
Then I write it, bit by bit,
Poetry-making is my *'bete-noir.'*
I do it every waking hour.
I sometimes wish that I could stop.
Is it pleasurable? It is not!
I wrestle with words and thoughts and
                                    vowels.
Frustration sometimes makes me growl.
I cannot find that special word
Which lifts the work from the absurd
And rests it on a higher plane
With all the fizz of best champagne.

P Reeves

ME MAM

I love me mam, she's small and sweet,
Search the world and you'll never meet,
A lady so serene and fine,
She's a little frail - well, she's eighty nine.

'Too frail to marry a farmer, dear,'
Her mother had said, or so I hear.
So she gave up teaching and, poorly wed,
Went on to raise six kids instead.

She was always there for me,
When I fell in the stream, or fell out of the tree.
So I thank the Lord that she's still alive,
I still need Me Mam - though I'm forty five.

Bruce Ward

FALLING DOWN BADLY
(For Stella)

I stumbled and your photo fell.
It fell from its place
propped there on the shelf.

I picked you up
as I did when you were two
and stood you back on your feet.
Back on your feet on the shelf.

Time was, when you fell a lot.
You fell on your knees and on your hands
and I always picked you up.

As you grew in years and wisdom,
You still fell.
You fell badly at times,
but you picked yourself up then.

You picked me up sometimes
because I fell too.
It seems like falling down
runs in the family.

But it's your turn now.
Your turn to pick up your child
and know the heartache
and pleasure of doing all that.

Now, you will know
just how hard it all is,
keeping your balance
in a world that's just made
to fall down in.

John Kandinsky

FRIDAY KNIGHT

Nightclub knight in crumpled armour
Gold medallion on his chest,
Watch him as he tries to charm her
Another damsel is distressed,

No castle now to store his gear
His wardrobe is a plastic bag,
Did he lose his Guinevere
Or did he leave his faithful nag,

Eau de brute he'd splashed under armpits
Now mixed with sweat has stained his shirt,
Then he spies a bird with big tits
Red fingernails to hide the dirt,

Over to her he will waddle
Ask her if she wants a drink,
Hello love are you a model
Eye to eye without a blink,

It will not matter if he loses
His foe is vanquished when he tries,
His sunbed tan will hide the bruises
The flashing lights will hide his eyes,

Pray tell sad knight what do you search for
On your Friday nightly quest,
Your battlefield the beer stained dance floor
With grail in hand your pint of best.

G Speakman

WITHOUT YOU

The cherry tree's in blossom now
It flowers every spring
I see the robins nesting and
I hear the blackbirds sing.
All these things still happen
Repeated every year
It doesn't seem to matter
To them, that you're not here.
They say that summer's coming
I say 'How can that be'
How can these things still happen
When you're not here with me.
We watched these things together
We shared the joys of life
You - my darling husband -
Me - your loving wife.
But you were taken from me
I'm so sad that you're not here
To see the new beginnings
The starting of the year -
How can life go on without you
The grief inside I cannot hide
You - so good - so enjoyed life
'It's not fair' I've cried and cried - but
All the sobbing - all the crying
Doesn't seem to change a thing
I'm alone - and have to face life
All that's left - a wedding ring -

Marion Smith

UNTITLED

Hate,
The cage,
Of greed,
Their breed,
Hidden,
Forbidden,
Reality,
Ignored,
The horde,
That scream,
For peace,
and justice,
Chained,
By the beast,
To toast,
The ugliness,
Released,
and join the crime,
Of greed.

K Pearce

NATIVITY

Under the pressure of Census call
Issued with Roman thoroughness to all,
When stately sages, riding in from afar,
Pass questing shepherds following a star,
One gentle creature, patient work well done,
Watches a mother with her infant son.
Only a donkey -
            yet as Mary sings,
Does he too recognise
            the Kings of Kings?

M M Burstow

SURPRISES

Life is full of odd surprises
Some are happy, some are sad
Some we wish we never had
But if we meet them with a grin
Take them squarely on the chin
They'll sure bring out the best within
Courage in troubles of our own
Kindness to another shown
Helps to oil the wheels of life
Easing pain and lessening strife
So let's endeavour day by day
To help another on his way
Then we'll find the pathway smoother
Just by helping one another
And at night as we seek our rest
Sleep well, having done our best

Katherine Larcombe

HURTING

I am hurting, deep inside me,
And I think you're hurting too.
But I believe the Lord will guide me;
Won't you let Him help you too?

When you feel your sorrows deeper
Than any pain you've ever known,
Stop; recall our Lord's own sorrow
Hanging on the cross, alone.

So bring the pain and the frustration
You feel you've bottled up inside.
Risen Jesus waits to heal you;
Loving arms are open wide.

Mary Petrie

TODAY'S DESPAIR

I once had a dream
and hoped it came true,
war had all ended and
       Love had shone through,
I dreamt men showed each other
       Love and respect,
they laid down their weapons
       and felt no regret,
Children grew up in a peaceful world
       they knew no words of hate
But then I awoke and saw it
       was too late.
I could hear a faint pitiful cry
I looked out of the window and saw
       a small boy,
they were calling him names because
       of the colour of his skin,
and on the TV I saw faces so thin,
the newscaster was telling of the
       third world,
baby's were crying through lack of food.
So I went back to bed and that
       night I cried,
I felt so useless, my hands were
       tied
I knew there was nothing I could do
       to put things right
Men would always raise their fists to
       fight,
There would always be hunger and poverty
And love and peace would never be
       free.

K Laskey

UNTITLED

Strip yourself naked,
      your clothes,
            your culture,
      your past.

Lay upon the forest floor,
      a leaf in one hand,
            earth,
                  clutched in the other.

A foot caressing the cold tingle of a gentle stream,
      eyes watching
            through the boughs,
clouds shifting the scenery of the sky,
      it remains,
            sky.

Nature abhors a vacuum they say

Nature seeks equilibrium they say

You, here on mother nature's breast
      in your nakedness
            are nature.

      Is it wrong then,

            to be what you are?

Ian Kirkpatrick

HEREFORDSHIRE

Neath the beauty of it's hillside,
Clad in rows of stately firs
Stretch miles of lush green farmland
Unspoiled through changing years.

The pleasant sounds of nature,
Reach out from wood and glade,
Wild flowers of rarest beauty
Are everywhere displayed.

I hear the cattle lowing
As they wander o'er the down.
The famous breed of Herefords
With hides all white and brown.

I see the quaint old houses
Grouped round in black and white,
Their gardens bright with snowdrops
And a cider press in sight.

I look towards the orchards
Where the cider apples grow,
And watch the winding river
In the valley far below.

I listen to the church bell
Ringing out in ancient spire,
A symbol of the peace that reigns
In this my Herefordshire.

Winifred Barber

COMRADES

I had a whim to plant a tree
when I was young;
and glad was I each year to see
its branches hung
with draperies of petals white,
then cherries red;
and year by year it grew in height
and wider spread,
until its canopies were laid
across the sky
in latticed veils of light and shade
to linger by. . .

Now here I sit below the boughs
on summer days,
in time's embrace, to dream and drowse
in sunlit haze
of splendid scenes of long ago;
those days serene
when fruit on bending boughs hung low,
and leaves were green.

Now are the branches gnarled and old,
crooked and bare;
and here and there are moss and mould,
where wintry air
has breached the leafless palisade.
Those urgent dues
to time, old tree, which we have paid,
none may refuse. . .

Edward Benbow

THE MEANING OF VEGGIE

The meaning of veggie is simple,
You say,
'You don't eat fish or meat,'
That is definitely true,
But there's much more to it than that.

We eat fruit, vegetables, nuts, rices,
Beans, pulses, wheats, and pasta too,
But at least we're kind to animals,
And the environment,
Which is more than I can say for you.

So don't underestimate veggies,
We're not the 'Birdseed Brigade,'
Just think about what you're doing,
And the price animals have to pay.

(Animals have a nervous system, so they
         can feel pain,
unlike vegetables. . .) Okay?

Kirsty Wilkes

INDECISION

A morning sun peeped round the door
Inviting him to play -
'Come out, come out, there's fun in store
I'm here to spend the day.'

Two tiny feet were hesitant
Though eager for a prank -
To dance with gems so brilliant
That sparked on dewy bank.

Behind him stood his birthday toys -
So bright, so gay, so new:
Before him stretched untrodden joys
Where pastures met the blue.

How could a little boy decide
Between pleasures men have made,
And pleasures *other hands* provide
Which time will never fade?

N M Beddoes

MEMORIES

Put me in the cupboard, Daddy, lock the door real tight.
I promise I won't call out when you switch off the light.
I like the silence in there, I like to be alone.
Going in the cupboard, I'm feeling quite at home.
The lock turns, and it's safe here, Daddy's got the only key,
and now he's going to the pub, so he won't be needing me.
Mummy shouts me through the door, 'I'd leave you there for days,
until you shrivel up and die, we'll see what Daddy says.'
Nanny talks to me one time, 'Don't believe what Mummy said,
Daddy will be home quite soon, he won't let you be dead.'
'I want to die though Nanny, before he turns the key,
before he tries to make me good, dead's what I'd like to be.'
'Don't be such a silly girl, you're only six years old.
Why do you say you want to die? Being dead is stiff and cold.'
I must be dead already then, at least some part of me,
I wonder, can you be quite dead just when you want to be?

G Arnold

OUR SHEILA

Off she went with here arm through Nanny's handbag.
Shoes like empty double-deckers, two angry bulls-eyes on her cheeks.
Slockety-clack, slockety-clack, she shuffled Japanese.

'What's that?' Mum grumbled into the sink.
'Just our Sheila with her arm through Nanny's handbag.'
'Then tell her to stop it. It's rude to look in bags.'
'Can't,' I said.

The peony hat had settled like a busby on our Sheila's button nose,
                               hiding the targets.
Her mouth was big and red as a letterbox.
Slockety-clack, slockety-clack, she slithered out of the gate.

'What you mean, can't?' Mum's knuckles moved, knobbly wet like the spuds.
'She's in the road'
'Then stop her stupid!'
Her voice went off like an alarm clock, her face went all folds and pinches,
                               and her lips went that dangerous white.

She wasn't hard to chase.
Slockety-clack, slockety-clack, blind but happy in that stupid hat.

The car *did* hit our Sheila but mostly Nanny's handbag.
It broke the glasses, bent the knitting and bounced our Sheila into touch.

Most of the bruises came from Mum,
A bran-tub of huggin' and bashin' while Sheila howled.

Weren't no way to end an outing.
She'd gone out as a grown-up
Slockety-clack, slockety-clack.
She was only a barefoot kid when she got back.

Penelope Weedon

FOR DEE

When sorrow laughs with the summertime fall,
By the grace of a child in a dreamer's grove -
As Nemesis grins at the theft of a soul
A lover glitters with a million more.
When violet rocks on the crest of a breeze
As tears are shed on a tender cheek
A life's desire is struck once more
By a passioned cry from a lover's court.
Speak love, cry love, kiss love, love,
Bloodstained visions, purple fears
The scream of a saint in another lover's ears
The rhythm of a witch, the dance round a flame,
The pleasure of sin
Dance through the cursed lands,
Caress the golden shore.
Dare to face the power of a lover's sword.

Joanne Smith

THE CHILD

A child is like a cloud
That floats into your life;
It passes by. . . it cannot stay,
Through the years of stress and strife,
It grows and blows away.

Fragile, pure and white,
It has no destination;
It drifts away. . . into the night,
Love, with no end,
But the final separation.

Mary South

THE TASK (SONNET ON A SONNET)

To distil feeling, capture sense, until
The very sap of truth begins to bleed
And burgeon from a single thought. The will
Is prisoner to the strict poetic creed.
What shall I do with all these fourteen lines
When I have nothing very much to say?
How did Yeats father something quite as fine
As Leda's form? - How did he pass this way?
Another quatrain, but where should I be?
No doubt some sort of climax neatly reached.
Revealed dimensions - rich economy?
Before his noble gift I stand impeached.
      This is the mould of masters, not of fools
      I have no right at all to blunt their tools.

Mary George

EASTER BOUQUET

Lovely April; earth reborn,
Winter's darkness turns to dawn.
Magic month - my heart is soaring
With the birdsong of your morning.

Budding twig and pale green shoot
From hidden bulb and buried root
Burst through tombs of earth to flower
And drink life-giving April's shower.

Lambs are dancing in green fields,
The brittle egg new life reveals
As Easter chicks break shell, to show
What lifeless seems, may not be so.

The dark seed planted in the earth
Awaits the Spring to give it birth,
Then April speaks from every flower
The truth of resurrection power.

Dorothy Avent

MEMORIES OF THE THIRTIES

Memories? - They're what you've left
When, of your youth and strength bereft
Your mind casts back to former days
With unashamed nostalgic gaze.

Old age tears holes in memory's net
But some things one cannot forget
No rockets went to Moon or Mars
When only *toffs* had motor-cars.

Woodbines in little paper packs
Five for twopence, including tax
Fry's chocolate came in penny bars
And Virol in Ali Baba jars.

No plastic bags the hedgerows filled
But all the little song-birds trilled
No litter in the streets was seen
And no graffiti marred the scene.

No yobbos then came into sight
The streets were safe to walk at night
But I am glad I'm seventy-one
For now those better days have gone.

Arthur Greene

THE CURRENT ATTRACTION

The nomadic conjurer traipsed into the village
Peddling his captivative enchantments.
The barren land made fertile by his arrival
Simmering with a pregnant air of anticipation
His intentions purely pleasurable.

His engaging appearance comes to life at night as his
Powers of irresistible seduction turn on.
I wait in the enclosure of darkness
Yearning for the thrill guaranteed by this good time lad.
Groups with girlish giggles cling to metal bars
Like pieces of glitzy gold trapped in plastic bags
Waiting to be won.
Menaced men mercilessly aim at tin ducks
Who taunt and tease, until hit.
I pay for my pleasure and roll up, roll up for a ride.
I hold on tight as reality dissolves around me, and any
Hostile faces blend into a sickly mass of colour
Waltzing faster and faster
A vomit verging, back breaking, neck aching, terror faking
Twist.

The fling ends.

Pressed up against the penny falls, but the penny doesn't drop.
The morning after, the scene has altered,
I see the peeling paintwork, tarnished mirrors and cracked bulbs
Unpleasant remnants of the dirty weekend.
He packed his bags, moving on for a repeat performance
Removing his spell from the land
Leaving it more desolate than before.
the only souvenir a tattoo on the earth,
No hearts or flowers, just a scar which will fester.

Leesa Rumley

THE DEATH OF A CHERRY TREE

How glad I am that every spring
We've taken snap-shots of the tree
Each year increased in blossom till
The branches curved and touched the grass,
A double-cherry flowering pink
Flamboyance, thirty springtime's sum
Of growing till this year - it dies.

The garden birds will miss it most
The sparrows and the chaffinches;
Blue-tits who in the winter would
Wait in it till we strung them nuts.
Magpies and crows have tested it,
Two collared doves have sheltered there.
Sometimes, a jay has flashed its blue
Amongst the branches rise and fall
And once, we thought a sparrow-hawk
Alighted, but so fleeting that
We were not sure of it at all.

Bright air balloons, an airship once
Appeared above its pale pink mass.
We stood within its shadow with
Our faces tilted skywards as
We watched them through the foam of flowers.

Mercifully, when it came down
We were out shopping in the town
Returning to a two foot scar,
A smudge of brown upon the grass.
Our very puzzled tabby stopped
With paw upraised in middle stalk
For scratching posts don't often walk!

Flora Owens

INNER MIND

Inner mind, inner space,
A land of dreams
A place that exists between waking and sleeping,
A land in which,
Surrealism becomes reality,
And elephants float,
Through a sea of ideas
Peanut butter pigs,
Talk with newspaper snails,
In the land where fiction becomes fact,
And anything goes, thoughts become matter,
Where everything and nothing can be trusted,
And everything and nothing can't,
Who knows what is around the next corner?
Who can tell what is going to happen in the past?

Chris McKenna

THE MEANING OF LOVE

Love is love
And love is living
Falling out
And then forgiving
Love is life
In all its beauty
Love is making love a duty
Love is laughing, crying, singing
Happiness to others bringing
Love is what makes the world
               go round
Love is happiness abounding.

W Causer

SPRING IN WILTSHIRE

We'll take a trip to Chippenham
That lovely Wiltshire town,
With its people kind and friendly,
And a market of renown.

Where Avon's flow serenely ranks
With fields of elms, green,
While willows grow along the banks,
The swans complete the scene.

The linnet's trill near Lowden rill
Will cheer us on our way,
And the hospital on Rowden Hill
A visit we will pay.

Then down the steep road that leads
Around the old stone wall.
Aroused from sleep, the squirrels leap
Amid the chestnuts tall.

The town has little changed, I think,
Since first I came this way.
A subway now is there to link
The shops, more bright and gay.

The grand old bridge has been replaced
By one more low and wide,
Which has encountered and embraced
The river's flow and tide.

No other place that I have seen
Has memories more dear,
So, when the springtime comes, Kathleen,
Our footsteps you will hear.

Christiana Boyle

SPEAKING OUT

When I say I don't like porn
I can feel your scorn
Rising from your member
To assault my view,
Like what I said was a cue
To stand up and be abused,
By you who think that to
cause a stink or even to think
Is a sin against you. Your liberty.
Oh, to have the nerve to stand up and say;
Don't dehumanise
Don't objectify
It affects me.
Me!
A person.
Not a mother, not a wife, not a prostitute, not a virgin, not a daughter
But a woman
Undivided.
Who doesn't like to walk into a newsagents
Or switch on a TV
And find men creating women in an image all of their own,
That has nothing to do with sexuality or expression or me.
You just want to put me down
In my place
To fill my face with your complete lack of grace.
Because you can't bear to see
What a real woman can be.
You can't stand to look at me
And to see me free.

Joanna Georgiades

THE STORY OF A NO-ONE

Here's the story of a no-one, someone no-one wants to know,
a thief, a liar, a scoundrel, the lowest of the low.
He will meet you walking down the street, or at a public bar,
with a hearty slap upon the back, he will ask you how you are,

So as not to seem unfriendly, you say, fine thanks, and you,
then you'll hear the patter of how the job fell through,
He's waiting for a giro from Social Security, but until it comes
on Friday he needs something to see him through.

You say okay, here's ten pounds but, let me have it back,
Oh, you'll have it back on Friday I can honestly promise you that
When Friday comes he's gone again as quickly as he came,
so's your money and everything you loaned him as a friend

Is this the last time you'll be caught, by a scoundrel such as he
I doubt it sir, very much, for the scoundrel, it is me,
The sooner the world realises there's no place for such as me.
There will be no more poetry written, for a simple nobody.

Thomas Hull

NEW DOOR

I'll walk down to the riverside and look back up to the hills
On days like today the clouds are grey and the wind blows some ill will
I shouldn't really be this way but some things feel so wrong
I've just heard the word about Cassy girl, someone just said she's gone
No-one knows what moves a soul to think such tragic things
But out of sight might mean respite from what desperation brings
The view of her world must have turned, rather like the sky today
More of just the bleak upon bleak, more grey fading into grey
I shouldn't really be like this, so much will be here soon
I push open a new door in life, while Cassy just left the room.

James Bull

UNTITLED

I have to be housebound
For a short while I hope
With time to spare
I sit and stare
With life everywhere
The wonder at the passing clouds
Sun now breaking through
Willow trees a weeping
With the host of golden daffodils

Women on their own
Holding children's hands
No man to share their burdens
For their love has quickly flown
Old age pensioners bustling by
With shopping bags to the full
Trying to survive.
But God knows where do they get the will
Up there, we hope it's heaven
Down here there is no
Peace on Earth!

Nora L Hanley

THE FLOWER GARDEN

A garden is a wonderful place,
To while away the hours,
There's peace and tranquillity all around,
As you sit amid the flowers.

The blooms are very beautiful
Their colours all so bright,
It gives you pleasure to be there,
From morning until night.

But think of the ones with sight impaired,
Whose beauty they cannot see,
And grow beds of lovely perfumed plants,
Like lavender, lilies and rosemary.

Mary E Goold

GREY

December's shroud of grey embrace,
Hides in mist, its greyest face.
The moaning fields of cold, grey earth,
Yearn to stir and wake to birth.
But flecks of grey float gently down,
Till the earth has donned its icy gown;
And all around, the winter's breath;
The touch of age, the kiss of death.

It only snows when the angels cry,
Dripping sorrow from the leaden sky.
Unanswered prayers that fall like lead,
Proclaim the message: God is dead.
Dreams of hope that are born tonight,
Can never hope to see the light,
For through this chill that'll never cease,
A grey dove flies in the face of peace.

And the winter's breath still closes in,
Breathing frost on our frozen skin.
Till this season's race is truly run,
These are the months of the vanquished sun.
We'll never be free of scenes like these -
The symptoms of this grey disease;
They'll haunt our dreams both day and night,
In this grey land of tainted white.

Vaughan Barnacle

AUTUMN

A land of cold winds and frosts
Outside the bitter winds,
Whistle through the naked branches of trees,
and underfoot the leaves are brown and crinkling.

A mist slowly descends, blanketing the world in silence,
and producing silver dew on the grass,
as one steps outside he sees the rotting leaves
and scents the herbaceous smell of autumn.

In the distance a little bird trills,
and one can hear the sound of a rake,
but even as leaves are gathered,
more leaves decide to drop.

Gold and yellows,
browns and dark green,
they stay barely
on their own separate branches.

And overnight,
a frost slowly comes on,
but by next afternoon, it is - all gone.

It created lovely patterns,
in a beautiful glittering white,
and covered the grass, with so it seemed,
silver glinting light.

But now - not a sign of it left,
except the wet, brown earth,
and the sheer beauty
of Autumn.

Mark Clemmow (12)

UNTITLED

No-one notices the old man
Totally ignoring him if they can
But what secrets does he keep
While on the park bench trying to sleep
Only he knows about giving out the order
On some foreign shell blasted corner
To charge out at the hidden enemy
That nobody can see
One by one his soldiers do fall
The remaining ones in a hole they crawl
They stick it out as long as they can
Now as leader he has to be a brave man
So from the front he leads the charge
Disregarding any obstacles or barrage
He carried on till the town is won
The enemy surrendering one by one
Another foreign town finds peace
Well for them at least
He must go on to fight more battles
Till the war is over and then enemy rattled
Quietly stepping back on civvies street
Telling no-one of his brave feat
He thinks only of his buddies that fell
Who fought so bravely and so well
Looking through his empty bottle of cider
At his medal that is a reminder
Of his fearlessness of the past
And to whom society make him an outcast
No-one notices the old man
Totally ignoring him if they can

F J Wilkes

MY FRIEND

I have a little dog
A very special dog
His name is Henri
And he is very friendly

When I am feeling blue
I say 'Hey you'
We need a walk
And a good talk.

When we have wandered
For a while
We are greeted with a smile
Some wish us good day
As we stroll on our way

There are some who wish to chat
The dog loves that as he gets a pat
We hear the news
And people's views
And I do believe I've lost the blues

Into a field we sometimes stray
Henri loves to roll in the hay
He really does enjoy his play
Of which he partakes every day

Down a shady lane we often go
Where he will run to and fro
When I decide to take a seat
I find him curled up at my feet

When there is a knock
Upon the door
He jumps around to let me know
Although his bark is rather loud
Of my little dog I'm very proud.

V Mann

YEAR OF THE CHILD

This is the year of the child
Whether they be innocent and mild
or they be rough and wild.
This year is for the child
In every street, town or country
Rich, poor or starved
help the child
for they are our future.

There are children in this world
Who are dying of hunger
No clothes to keep them warm
No shoes on their feet
Their eyes full of tears
that wonder.

Others have a home, toys and nice things
They have plenty to eat, money for a treat,
But are given keys to let themselves in
No-one home all alone
Instead of love they have other things

We find babies on door steps
Left wet and cold
No mother's love, no arms to hold
Let this be the year of the child
Let us all help these innocent children
They did not ask to go through all this
God Bless you children
For you are our future.

Helen Rands

CONFIDENCES

saddened
by stuttering truth
     the fresh pain

mismatched they bring each other down

'I told him the truth
was honest
of my dishonesty'

     by consequence
too much was said
the deed spilt old deeds
dragged from hiding
     emotions
under the microscope
but truth is good

     truth implodes
a clean breast is a bloody affair
anger dredges up the past
cutting off all exits.

Caroline Owen-Thomas

HOME AGAIN

Once more the key turns, lets me in
To quiet silence - like the grave.
I must not falter, those who watch
And wait, to see how I behave!

Though I am truly all alone,
I feel and sense that *she* is there
All silent are the TV and the phone.
Perhaps I'll ring, do not despair!

Search as I may, all numbers blur.
Pages will not turn, as fumbling finger's shake.
Slowly the sadness rises, reality
Takes a hand, the call I cannot make!

But help, always close by for all,
Perhaps the Vicar at the Rectory?
Those quiet reassuring words, 'My boy
The number for Heaven, is ex-directory!'

T G Bloodworth

UNTITLED

If you have a secret,
And keep it to yourself,
It will still remain a secret,
And kept within yourself.

If you can keep the secret,
And feel at peace within,
You can hold onto the secret,
And live your life within.

If the secret holds for you,
The key to someone's pain,
Let go of your secret,
And let the sun remain.

The release of your secret,
Brings love to someone near,
To sacrifice your secret
Gives peace to someone dear.

Angela Wellings

JOURNEY OF LIFE

A shadow spreads over the fields of green,
The sun is hidden, the grass hardly seen;
The colour changed to a darker shade -
What difference the loss of sun has made.

The pretty patchwork fields are shrouded now
With floating mist and cloud, and hardly show -
Until at length the welcome sun peeps through
And they once more come racing into view.

This country scene speaks of our way through life -
Some days are filled with joy, others with strife:
Sometimes the way is clear and all goes well,
Then trouble strikes us - why we cannot tell.

As sunshine's often followed by the rain
Our lives are changed by suffering and pain;
And loneliness can be a bitter blow -
Do not despair, although the way is slow.

For we are not alone, our friends do care
And they will listen and our burdens share;
The dark clouds will lift - in a little while
And God will look upon us with His smile.

Janice Fuller

TIME

Do we have time to put right this world
for all who will follow us, all boys and girls
What will we leave them to inherit from us
war and pollution, hatred no trust

We are the elders on whom they rely
What will we leave them? Dead earth, dead sky
Our earth is a wonder of life in itself
A gift for all beings, so full of wealth.

Do we destroy what nature has given
and take from our children this garden of Eden.
The seed in the womb is where all life starts
With the shaping of the body, and the beating of the heart

The birth of a child is as a seed in the earth
as it breaks through the soil to show us its worth.
Our pollution and rape will kill off these seeds
and the wild life will vanish because of our greed.

Our nature has changed from that of a child
as our needs are more desperate for the more we desire
Greed is a killer that we must all destroy
Its vast hand of destruction waiting to deploy
Our earth must remain as nature intended
For the children of our children, as their garden of Eden.

J M Lewis

THE BOX

We're sitting in silence, nobody talks,
The dog looks dejected - don't get his walks,
Dishes are piling up in the sink,
Don't know what will happen if one needs a drink.
The phone never rings, and nobody calls.
Wallpaper is hanging off of the walls.
Don't dare to move or someone pinches your seat
Feeling quite hungry - but there's nothing to eat.
Outside there is chaos - what do we care.
We'll stay where we are secure in our chair.
Away from all trouble, strife and melee,
And carry on with our pastime.
            Just watching the telly!

Gladys Locke

THE HOMELESS MAN AS SEEN THROUGH
A RESTAURANT WINDOW

I watched you, yesterday,
through a window.
You wrapped yourself in rainbows,
your dog whining pathetically;
tail
  like
    a burnt
      French fry.

Our eyes met
over my hamburger, and you
looked at me.
Not a sad look,
but proud, proud.
And you lay down in the rain,
there and then,
as if it deserved you.
And your dog curled around your legs
as you both closed your eyes
and slept.
Or made a pretence at sleep.
And I watched you,
as I ate
  my hamburger,
    my American fries,
     my doughnut,
       my ice-cream.

And I wondered about the end of the world,
and whether it was coming.
And whether it had come.

Sarah Mooney

BLUE RINSE AND CURLERS

Indiscriminately dissecting the lives of those
Round them, they sit beneath hairdryers - judges elect.
The evidence comes from Mrs Jones' rumour,
Was it him, was it her? Well now I forget.
Scandal abounds with the blue rinse and curlers
Behind twitching curtains each wait like a spy,
'I hear Mr Davies has got a new girlfriend.'
'Are you ready yet Audrey? Oh yes, nearly dry.'
Out come their photos of numerous grandchildren
Each face looks suspiciously just like the first.
The stylist runs out of comments to make now. Sighs
of relief when each pulls out their purse.
And so they return to their different houses on
Different roads and different streets. All
Icy cold and equally empty.
The next time they see someone? Just a matter of
Weeks.

Karan Round

ETERNAL

Why do you cry my precious?
Lift up your eyes, and see this everlasting
life, that God has given me.
Feel my love embrace you, in the warmth of
Summer breeze,
Hear my tender whisper, in the rustle of the trees,
See my smile, in starlight, and the glow of golden sun,
Dry your tears my darling, my spirit still
lives on.

Catherine Whyley

TIME TO TURN

Let me tell you this tale of growing old
And the passing of eternal time,
How a blink of God's eye is your time here
On Earth,
So is it really all worthwhile?
From the cradle to the grave is a moment
To reflect,
That decisions taken in haste,
Have a habit of hurrying back to haunt -
Even the human race.
Take time to think, and reflect a while,
As you grow old and grey,
That a blink of your eye is all it takes,
To change your mind today.

Charlotte Salter

GRATITUDE - SOLD

To Clark's shoes
I owe a debt of gratitude,
for as a child
running wild,

see we're a pretty big family,
when light dawned on a fresh new day.
I had one pair of Clarks, no sir they weren't for play,
I cleaned them every night and only wore them Sunday.

In the week I had my bumpers, wellies, and lace-up plimsolls,
my pride, my joy, forget my favourite toy, my Clarks weren't full of holes,
ones with a compass could get you to the north pole.
When I wore them I was more of a rat than a vole.

P M Richards

WINTER
BENEATH THE SHADOW OF CHRISTMAS

Now the Autumn wind has gone
the Christmas season has begun
where through a Winter fog it shone
the flame red fire of our Sun
immersed in wisps of cotton clouds
a silent landscape so serene
crystal snowflakes formed white shrouds
where only trees are evergreen.

Icicles formed like tears of joy
from glistening drops of tumbling snow
and upon the face of a little boy
a warming smile a healthy glow,
for in this Winter wonderland
an ancient magic grips a child
the dream white topping is so grand
And Santa Claus is not defiled.

Beyond the meadows showered white
a frozen lake wears a translucent coat
the cold wind whispered in the night
to make this stream of ice remote
Creatures rest in natural bliss
fast asleep in the Winter cold
nature blessed this Earth with a chilling kiss
as Christmas Yuletide does unfold.

Far across this icebound glacial plain
where kindness of heart does reign supreme
shared thoughts of love will still remain
long after the thaw of this crystalline dream.

Gavin Paul Carter

IN PRAISE OF AMNESIA

Forget the past
As it is happening.
Imagination
Stems from the memory.
With no past there is no memory.
With no imagination there is no future.
Only an everlasting present tense
That lives without living
And exists
Solely because it must.

Peace is the eradication
Of memory and imagination.
The destruction of the soul.

Susan Francis

VOICE FROM THE GRAVE

Come now dear one,
To the dark side.
And drown your old life,
In a blood red tide.
To seek an endless romance
A never dying necromancy.
Voice from the grave.

Shadow that creeps the black slate,
Does not make a sound,
Hangs outside the window,
Let the stars fall to the ground.
The sky is slashed wide open,
So the city she spills out.
And like your rich red wine my love,
This wretch can't live without.
Voice from the grave.

Sleep softly in your deathbed dear,
With petals and vermin,   .
A new life nears.
Your beauty shall not fail you,
Until the virgin kill.
They will know not the dark reason
As to why life grows so pale.
Song from the grave.

Pete Coutts

THE MAN THAT NEVER WAS

As I stand on the lonely bridge
The lonely bridge of life
I pause to think, to memorise my troubles and my strife
As I stand here lost and alone - can't anybody see
The man that people thought I was just wasn't really me

For I am not the kind of man who people clearly see
Beneath the warm exterior lurks a fiend, that man is me
For I have lied and cheated, ruined your faith in all mankind
Another man my equal will be very hard to find
The things that I have stolen, the deeds that I have done.
I shouldn't be a free man, and that's why I have come

Now that it is much too late, too late to recompense
I've seen the error of my ways, at last I've seen some sense
So I will leave this lonely life, one step and I'll be free
Now the hate within me burns me up, for all to see
With me will go the evidence that even sickened me
For under the collection box, a plaque in ivory which reads
'In aid of Mary Watkins, who died aged only three.'

P Evans

BELIEVE

Your creation insults my intelligence.
Your knowledge insults my mind.
Your existence insults my presence.
Your beauty insults my eye.

My intelligence insults your creation.
My mind insults your knowledge.
My presence insults your existence.
My eye insults your beauty.

Your creation is in my intelligence.
Your knowledge is in my mind.
Your existence is in my presence.
Your beauty is in my eye.

Janine Kay

LIFE

Make the most of your life, you have only one,
enjoy it profoundly, but don't hurt anyone.
When life treats you right you have love and laughs,
lots of happiness flowing along your paths,
but you have to put in what you want to get out,
kindness and love is what it is all about.
Your sad days will come with its pain and sorrow,
but you will find the strength to start a new tomorrow.
Whatever the problem be it money or strife,
take a good look at the whole of your life,
be thankful for so many things that others have never had,
and store them in your memory for when you are feeling sad.
When you get old and can only reflect, your memories
are precious, so, make them perfect.

Marguerite Rose

YOU

Each day I wake and when I do
First thoughts that come to mind
                              are you
I say a prayer and when I do
I pray that He will care for you.
Care for you while you're away
Till you come back to me one day.
I work each day and when I do
My thoughts keep straying love, to you.
I know you had to go away
To foreign lands a while to stay.
I also know you took my heart
When you return, we'll never part.
I sleep each night and when I do
The dreams that come to me are you.
So waking, working, dreaming too
Love walks beside me, and it's you.

Margaret Walker

IN THE MORNING

See the wreckage of the night before;
The fags in the carpet, the puke on the floor,
Cones in the garden, a nicked traffic sign,
The sight of flat beer, the stench of stale wine.
The hideous girl, you can't remember.
The former friend, you tried to dismember.

Your head is pure pain,
You're throwing up bile,
Never again.

Or not for a while.

A P Shanks

131

BUGS AND BEASTIES

When hot and sultry we need the air,
But during Summer do take care,
As bugs and beasties of the night,
Creep into homes to find the light.

With open windows waiting there,
In they come to fright and scare,
All night we swat and then we spray,
Wishing they would go away.

They buzz and hover in the air,
Across the ceiling, everywhere,
Spiders run across our feet,
Looking for a quick retreat.

Moths flutter with delight,
Within the glare of the light,
Daddy longlegs hanging low,
Whizzing round to and fro.

At last to bed and even there,
A mosquito buzzes in the air,
Although it's hot, oppressive too,
Open windows will let them through.

So shut them tight,
Turn out the light,
Or bugs and beasties of the night,
Will come and visit you.

S Green

THE SILENT PREACHER

Oh Mother are you well?
I ask this so as not to offend,
For alas upon you, so many have fell,
Yet for life on you we depend,
But your children they plan such destruction,
From Eden on Earth lies great corruption.

I hang my head in mortal shame,
Yet still no end as we heap sin upon sin,
For your pain, we are surely to blame,
Is there no future for our solar dustbin.
Forgive me now, as I try not to falter,
Walk in your shadow, pray at your altar.

Now I give you a new child to cherish,
Help me in all, to teach and defend,
Fill him with light so bright not to perish,
Show him things of which there's no end,
For we are the pupils, you the lone teacher,
Yet still we won't listen to our silent preacher.

Darren Martin Williams

WHERE DID WE GO WRONG?

The constant pain of knowingly we worry and we try
To find the reason why, and let no-one see us cry
We've done our best to bring you up in honesty and truth
When you started bad we put it down to youth.
But teenage years are gone my son, and still you carry on
As if you couldn't care my son, please tell us where we're wrong.
To cope with sanity, turn away and hope, I shut my heart and mind
You never change, you lie, you steal, always revert to kind.

Janet Thornton

LITTER LITTER

Litter here, litter there,
Litter litter everywhere.

Litter on the playground,
Litter in the woods,
Litter on the footpath
Litter in my boots.

Litter on the highway,
Litter on the beach,
Litter in the meadows
Litter at my feet.

Litter from my pocket,
Litter from my shirt,
Litter from McDonalds
Lands up in the dirt.

Litter all around us,
Litter needs to go,
Litter needs a place to rest,
In the bin it goes!

Selina Corradi (11)

IN MEMORY
(To my wife, on the death of my father)

So limpid let the dewfall of thine eye
Rest gently in the dawn of this thy grief
Until the callous sun brings noon's relief
And all the high downland of thy mind be dry.

Plead not with me that I should with thee lie
In woods where only thou canst feel the leaf
Of mourning fall, his autumn's brief
Caprices winter stopped, when all things die -

And I, on seeing frozen clay, am cold;
What dew I had has long since turned to frost.
His summer's mellow harvest has been lost
On broken straws; the trampled corn grown old.

Reap lonely then thy comfort in grief's field;
Leave me to drink the gall remorse must yield.

James Burgess

LIMPLEY STOKE

I remember when it first began.
The end of a hot summer's day
we stood above the valley;
you watched the trains
snake slowly on their way
to Dorset county and the sea
whilst I saw the moon
full and steady above the
dark of the valley hillside.
Nobody there in the hotel grounds
no person sitting beneath
the Cinzano umbrellas.
We watched, shadows of
a former age,
suddenly I felt a
great surge of affection
and you transmitted to me
a message of real desire.

Joan R Gilmour

THE FOUR SEASONS

In Spring, flowers open wide,
Children laugh and play outside.
In Summer, people go to the beach,
And feel the sand run through their feet.

In Autumn, leaves fall from the trees,
In that cold and windy breeze.
In Winter, we might have snow,
Some people want it to last, some to go.

After all that happens,
It starts all over again.
Will it all be different,
Or, the same.

Laura Corradi (9)

THE FOG HORN

I hear the fog horn blowing
The haunting sound so knowing
It echoes that it's bad at sea
And very lonely just like me.

On a night like this I'd rather be
Sitting down long side the sea.
Although the view would be rather bleak
It's only the peacefulness I seek

It makes it easy for me to think
Where sleep's concerned it's just a blink
I'm like a ship lost in the night
Struggling through till it gets light.

Diane Bennett

MY BEST PAL

Them dogs
They always want walking
They're a best pal
For talking
Never tell a secret
That's so true
I can assure you
Never hate you
Always glad
To see you
No matter
How long you have been away
Every day
They're always happy
Never *ever* cry
They love you all the world
They hate to say goodbye
They come everywhere
With you
Never dare
To leave your side
Never go to sulk
Or cry
When they are old
And have to die
It breaks your heart
To leave their side
They will always
Be in your heart
So you may never part.

Jessica Price (10)

THE VISION OF DEATH

Immortal soul, where dost thou lie?
The body rots beneath the stone;
I am, oh God, so much alone,
Why do I live, why did he die?

The dusk surrounds the gravehead cold,
And gloomy hangs the yew behind:
Death's silent sentinel, unkind
And grasping, living, yet so old.

I thought I chanced to see a form -
An image of the one death took -
His face was like an open'd book,
But hard to understand, and torn

Out was the page of Life,
And in its place a deathly veil
Choking the words behind with pale
Oblivion; yet came a knife

A sentence sharp - the words were clear -
To comfort me and soothe, and then
The old expression flashed again
Before the book was closed for e'er.

The vision fades - I see the tomb,
He lies at rest, his life was good,
His spirit soars, and never could
I sorrow now - Death is no doom.

Jenny Duckworth

FOREST SKETCHES

Alone in the deep woods;
Primeval silence;
Greenness all pervading.
Sunlight, flecked with whirling dust;
A kaleidoscope of leaves.

An irregular lattice of oak columns,
Mossy and deeply furrowed;
Crawling ant hills amongst dense ferns;
A narrow path almost buried beneath leaves.

A gale shrieks through the woods,
Like a siren warning of destruction.
Trees moan and creak,
Their crowns sent twisting and swaying.

A bloated stream seethes in its gorge,
Its foam streaked waters the colour of soil.
A fallen branch, lodged between rocks,
Makes a weir for the roaring torrent.

Autumn has kindled the forest,
The beeches blaze orange and red;
Oak leaves, bronze and crisp,
Rustle in the wind, but refuse to fall.

I see an even flow of leaves,
Softly piling layer upon layer;
Like semi-floating flakes of consciousness,
Lost and doomed to die.

All is silent, but for birds,
And the rippling of a stream,
The powder barks of enmeshed conifers
Are mottled with sunlight.

A R Chadwick

BRISTOL CHANNEL MAN

I'm your Bristol Channel man,
I go sailing when I can,
Whenever the wind blows free,
But I'm sitting on the mud,
Waiting for the flood,
Dreaming of the deep blue sea.

I'm a special sort of cove,
With an urge that wants to rove,
The salt in my blood runs free,
So I'm working on my boat,
And I know it's going to float
And take me to the deep blue sea.

I've got a lifeboat off a ship
And now I'm letting rip,
And setting my fancy free,
I've nailed up every hole
And put concrete in the sole,
As ballast for the deep blue sea.

Oh, the superstructure's fine,
It's got me in every line,
With plywood I've been quite free,
It's got portholes alfresco,
And the doghouse is just so,
To keep off all that deep blue sea.

Mind, she lets the water in
but it runs back out again,
My money I'm spending free,
And she's really taking shape,
and I've bought adhesive tape,
Getting ready for the deep blue sea.

You may think it very odd
That I need no sign from God,
But my soul is sailing free,
When I'm dreaming of my boat,
And how she's going to float,
And take me to the deep blue sea!

R S King

LIFE

Along life's highway we all go
Some pass quickly, some pass slow
We all see the sky of blue
The fields of green, the morning dew
The sun, the moon, the stars at night
They are there for our delight
Birds and beasts, the flowers too
They are here to walk with you.

Along life's highway we all go
With sun and wind, rain and snow
Hold in your hearts the things you see
The stately swan, the humble bee.
The swallows flight, the curlews call
The butterflies, the oak trees tall
Life is so short, so hold on to
The gifts that nature give to you.

Along life's highway you did go,
Did you learn? Do you know?
Why were you even here at all?
Did you stumble? Did you fall?
If not, I ask you one last thing,
Was your life, worth living?

R Nightingale

THE MAGIC OF NOW

I do not join contemporaries who dip
Nostalgically in rainbow yesterdays,
Unless I wish to raise a rueful smile.

I will not summon up a squandered youth
Much better left behind. Well do I know
That backward glances there will bring no joy.

But now, past three score years and ten I've found
Rich, unalloyed and inexhaustible,
Treasures undreamed of in my callow years.

I have discovered art - my own weird brand of it,
A world emerging from some secret place
In tumbling words, in sculpture and in paint.

Belated I step outside my head
To give my three eccentric friends, knife, brush and pen
Their unique chance to practise there unchecked.

Whatever critics say, I pay no heed.
My friends' monstrosities I love, I am their slave.
My eager hands obey their every whim.

At their command colours, shapes, words jostle
In the limbo of my mind for being,
And I, and only I, can give them life.

In tactile hymns my fingers sing their birth,
And singing still, they praise that random light
Which floods with gold the Autumn of my days.

Betty Hancox

142

NEXT DOOR

They're digging again next door
I can hear them
straining

It's night and it's getting darker
I can't see them
scraping

I know they're whispering about me
They've seen me
watching

The wind moans my name through the window
It's cracked
chilling

I long for the sound of a scream
of a fight
resistance

But everything's kept under wraps
repressed
smothered

And my heart beats in time to the footsteps
of death
approaching.

Alan Jacobs

HAPPINESS OR YUPPY-NESS

Here I am once more,
Trying to change the score.
Yet again I'm sitting here,
On another day
In another month
Of a boring year.
Nothing's happening here.

I'm trying to set the pace,
From the wrong end of the race.
It's not that I'm unaware,
It just seems that way
'Cos I've got nothing to say
Till the end is near.
Nothing's happening here.

You've done it all before,
And yeah, you've seen it all I'm sure.
But if you think there's nothing new,
Then you'll just fade away
To a duller grey
Than you were before.
Just another closed door.

I cannot comprehend,
Why you think you don't need friends.
It's not against the law,
But if you fly alone
Then you'll die alone
And there's nothing more.
Just another closed door.

Don't worry about your face,
Come and join the human race.
Stop thinking about the time
Just relax for a while
And try to paint on a smile.
Use a different line.
Being you's not a crime.

M Plowman

SELF ADOPTED

I orphaned myself
Rejecting my external mother
Obliterating my gran
I cowered in a piteous pit
hoping to be rescued
and given love and life
I glued myself to others
for security and consistency
each time they left
I shrivelled away
I can now reach out
asking for guidance
to structure my life
I'm beginning to reach inside me
and nurture my child Nicola,
with unconditional love
for my maternal Nicola
I can begin to adopt myself
for many years to come
learning to accept and love me as I am
and help me to learn to live
for today.

N Linfield

THE LOSS OF THE SILVER GALLEON
(Christmas '93, a brain haemorrhage took Andree
my only female friend and my partner, Bobbie's kindred spirit.
Both of the moon, their silver binds them forever.
For me, and her husband, Doomsday end)

Breathless he stood, etched grey with fatigue and desolation.
The curlew unwittingly cracks the silence around waterlogged feet.
Black shadowed cormorants perceive, sidelong, his swaying motion.
Standing now, he trespassed inside her, voiceless unable to greet.
Her black Spanish hair no longer stallion bright, clings to her high-boned
cheek,
the persistent mistral, for all its devotion, concedes defeat.

Through searing scream she set sail without us, at sunless dawn.
Naked, we clung to each other, as demons tapped at panes.
Only three horsemen now, dance and ride on the rack of reminiscence.
Clutching at the rib *He* took once before, they challenge alchemy to restore.
But only one is wrapped in the silver embrace, of the butterfly
wings of the Silver Galleon.

She, through her unyielding faith, spins the silver gossamer lace,
which girds the unicorn she rides to make the secret feel,
of breath on face.
In twilight fields poppies bow, stand aside, and congratulate,
two true friends in this spiritual place.
Hark! The silver bell. No others longer hear nor see, 'tis just the
Silver Galleon, of Bobbie and Andree.

Jack Ward

SWEET MUSIC IN THE TOWN

It's so clear, that dignified old man has seen better days
As he sits with his harp, in the high town and plays

In old fashioned tall hat, and, frock coat grey
Playing sweet music as we pass on our way.

146

To my child's mind, it's so sad, that he has to sit there.
For I feel it's not right, in the evening air.

He belongs in a more gracious time
Playing while ladies take afternoon tea
Not for these uncaring people, rudely, pushing past me.

They don't seem to hear, that sad melody,
Singing from the old harp's heart, so sweet,
I vow to bring him a penny next time we meet.
But, in vain, I look for him now, at the coffee shop door
For Winter has come and I see him no more.

Eva Sutherland

SEASONS

How sad to think a summer bloom
Can fade into the gathering gloom.
A flower that shone as bright as day
Has withered now, into decay.
The beauteous rose I longed to hold,
Its promise richer far than gold,
Has treated my approach with scorn,
Rejecting love's hand with its thorn.

The season's change means hope must die.
Too long now have I lived a lie,
And winter's desolate, dreary theme
Can overcome a long-held dream,
For summertime has loved and lost,
And by the winter storms we're tossed.
We travelled through the autumn rain,
But never will see spring again.

Jeff Rawlinson

COUSIN CALIBAN

Caliban's creed is what man is made of
The South wind chides mortals with
Whispers of ghosts,
Demons, mermaids and fairies.
Though snakes and toads fawn at his feet
Caliban's realm is of a parallel dream.
Does not man grovel beneath the idol?
Marvellous the beast of human creation,
Noble creature, kith of man.
So beauteous when enraged.
So pitiful in servility.
My soul's teacher.
Caliban.

Holly Claire Lewis (16)

AUTUMN BEACH

Here rolling waves unfurl
As foam-edged ripples slide and curl
Shingled seaweed mounded high
Leaves shining sand bared to sky
While keening wind cuts right through
November skies translucent blue
And bare-limbed, dry-leaved trees
Cling crazily
On crumbling cliffs and sliding screes

The seas and sands and winds of being
Shape my life beyond my seeing
Clinging to the cliffs I strive
To keep the inner light alive.

M E Lloyd

UNTITLED

A bird enslaved in a not so gilted cage
Found she could not fly or sing
Discovered she alone held the key
Opened the lock and took wing.

Far she flew and much she saw
And soon she learned to sing
Sweeter grew the melodies
And joys the song did bring

To some the key is easy found
To all it lies within
To search for where the key is forged
The journey can begin.

The lock is never far away
But the key is hard to turn
To study what has gone before
Is where one starts to learn

And in that not so gilted cage
Another bird looks on
And sees a soulmate flying high
Away into the sun

And key in heart he struggles hard
So much he needs to fly
To learn the song we all must sing
Before we're fit to die.

Scott Court

EIGHT MONTHS ON

So it's been eight long months
Since I wrote those lines
Since those summer times
When the balloons were sailing,
And I made my way
Up old Cherhill
To think of the day,
My eyes still gaze
But now with knowing,
For I made the move
Towards that woman,
Came to know
Her life and reason,
For the way she looked,
Confused and hidden,
How the husbands had
Simply trodden
On the plans she made,
And now with children
She's seen men's looks
And heard their promise
Of undying love, and future bliss,
Even though I thought I was different
And said,
She left for peace, contentment
And Holyhead!
Those natural children,
Secure to grow
In a place they know and call
Their home,
So we never flew kites, balloons or walked,
On that lonely old Iron-age fort,
But in years to come
As an independent bloke,
I'll think of her and remember
That I wrote
Because we made the effort,

We met and spoke,
Put it all on hold, ignored the stares,
Really held her close and told her there's
Someone right here who wanted it told,
He wouldn't miss those months
For the world.

R Kallet

EVEREST

Along the winding path I tread,
Each shallow step in snow, I dread,
A hidden danger to traverse
A rock or crevice, or even worse.

A deathly roar, ice falls so near,
The mountain's curse, rings in my ear,
The path grows narrower, danger rears,
A laboured breath, aching, fears.

The cry of 'Avalanche' rings out,
'Take Cover' is the awesome shout,
A cleft in the rock, my body to hide,
Safe from the mountain's destructive tide.

The roar of destruction abated, peace,
Sunlight and snowflakes, clouds like fleece,
The top of the world, Heaven's gate to touch,
Breathless astonishment, beauty, hushed.

Philip Tittensor

UNTITLED
(To Robert, Elizabeth, Jenny, Edward, Tammy and the others)

Your existence was brief but treasured
And your presence was felt almost at once
You will always be part of my body and soul
Though I never saw you or cuddled you close

I picture you all in a meadow
Beside a babbling brook
Laughing and playing together
Patiently waiting for us to appear

Sleep peacefully my most wanted treasures . . .

Sally Hopkins

THE GARDEN

Wander along the garden path,
Arching roses overhead;
Pinks and violets beneath.
As you pass,
Crickets jumping in the grass.
Hearken to the birds that sing.
Nurtured on nearby nettles,
A butterfly settles,
Choosing his favourite flower.
Hover flies and bees content,
From hosts of blooms breath in the scent.
In harmony with all around,
Peace is found.

Ann Forrest

ADAM'S ROSE

Old Adam lived deep in the woods,
A hermit's life he led,
With beard that came below his waist,
Well, that's what people said,
The birds all tried to build their nests,
In that grey beard, so long,
They all were fed, by bits of bread,
And thanked him with a song,
The rabbits brought their babies,
To Adam's broken door,
He picked them up and loved them,
And they came each night for more,
The squirrels brought their nuts to him,
As if to share their food,
A fox would sit down by his side,
Or roll in playful mood,
He loved the beauty of each flower,
Those stars that shone by night.
The moon high in the heavens,
That, was his guiding light,
When every season came around,
In turn they brought him joy,
For each had happy memories,
When he was just a boy,
He knew that God created all,
Those things he held most dear,
And with a faith so steadfast,
Then nothing did he fear,
And when at last, the old man died,
No creature could be found,
But where the old home had once stood,
A rose sprung from the ground.

Mollie Sage

HIGH STREET CHIPPY

Fish and chips, patties too,
Take your place
In the queue.
Money ready,
Give your order,
The queue is almost
Round the corner.
For you, Sir,
Fish and chips, patty too,
Splash of vinegar,
No salt for you.
Our pies and sausages
Are tasty too.
For Madam,
Peas, just a few,
Fish cake twice,
And a burger too.
He batters more fish
As his customers wait,
He will serve them all
Before it gets late.
As the last customers dwindle away,
He closes his doors
On another busy day.

Kenneth W Bishop

THE WOOLLY FLOCK

O' lonely sheep in the meadow green,
grazing in sweet content
feeding the frisky woolly lambs
showing them how your days are spent

Oft have I watched you at your play
frisking and jumping and tearing around,
leaping over each others' backs
amusement and joy with the flock I found.

White woolly lambs and darker sheep
what are your thoughts in the pastures fair
do you have moods like the human race
docile and gentle, or feelings laid bare.

Here you are now standing out in the rain
looking bedraggled with wet woolly backs
huddling together to try and keep warm
sheltering the lambs 'neath your cuddly necks

Now I must drag myself back to work,
watching the flocks makes my thoughts run astray,
how can I start on my daily tasks when I'm counting the
sheep by night and by day.

Jeanne Martin-Tammas

THE FISHERMAN'S TALE

Three fishermen sit talking
Of catches made that day
And how the blue sea calls them
In her quiet seductive way

She calls to say she needs them
To come and talk at night
And whisper soft sweet nothings
Beneath the still moonlight

They know she will always own them
And that they will never be free
For they are bound by tides of blue
To their mistress called the sea.

D A Borge

AFTER SIX WEEKS' DROUGHT

The rain slips sensuously,
Slowly, softly, silently,
Sinking into the soil
That's been saddened
By neglect and toil.
The birds are singing, gladdened
That breakfast worms abound
- Ready meals again around.
Grass gracefully gradually grows
Greatly, gloriously growing again.
Thanks to the beloved rain.
Seeds that the sower sows
Swell and soon will germinate
Thankful of their happy fate
That now they need not be too late
For harvesting at some future date.
Fruit will have its flavour freshened
Flowers' fragrance will not be lessened
Animal and bird, insect and grub
Rejoice, rejuvenated by Life's hub
Thankful Life can live again
- All due to precious *Rain*

Judy Allen

WHERE DID OUR TIME GO?

Where did our time go?
We were young and so free;
We laughed at our dangers
We laughed, you and me.
We played with our shadows
And the sun always shone
'Til time came and stole
All our chariots of fun.

The candles are dimming
On our joyous hall,
Full of light, full of friendship
Now were starting to fall,
To the jaws of the beast
Which is lurking outside,
No point in running
There's nowhere to hide.
It's coming to get us,
To grasp, chew and spit,
'Til reshaped we appear
In a bottomless pit.

Where did our time go?
We reached for the stars,
But now we just sit
And look out of the bars!

Jan Ralph

1946 - 1995

Goodbye was said aeons, aeons ago
When soft eyes melted war embittered heart.
Though each perceived the other as a foe
And thought it right that enemies should part.
Through fifty years that ever fixed mark
Fused by the poet in the soul of each
Has nurtured a divinely glowing spark
Searching across the miles and years to reach.
Sweet comfort give and comfort take
For all the bruises of a heart bereft,
Each to help each a loving life to make
Although the life of each was sorely cleft.
        Thus may a love which life can never test
        Rise up and grow, and shadow all the rest.

Hazel Browne

OKEHAMPTON CASTLE

The cold
upon the hill
The stone
that gives a chill
The shadow
of the walls
The dark
of all the halls
The dungeons
misty and blank
The smell
of musk and dank
The castle
all in all
Is one
great Heaven hall

Ian Harris

MY BEAUTIFUL GOD

You are like a morning song
That lifts hearts on high
Uplifts us from the daily gloom
You point us to the sky.

The Holy One is near
No sin in Him is found
The power of the Lord
It's found in all our prayers
Moving in this place
We worship Him

The end will come
As the trumpet blows
The Father of us will appear
We will be afraid to look
God in His face
Yes, Judgement Day is here.

Bill Graham

MEMORIES

It's autumn in the park,
Leaves crunch to powder underfoot
As I walk alone,
Thinking of you:
Your hair, your eyes, your smile;
Cheeks that glowed tulip red
Now so pale and still.
It's autumn in the park,
But winter in my heart.
I feel so cold and numb,
I can't believe you've gone:
Your hair is in the squirrel's tail,
Your eyes in the blue, deep sky.
My cries are in the lost lamb's wail:
Why can't I join you - why?
The snow blankets the hill
Like the cold layer round my heart,
I can hear your whisper still -
You said we'd never part.

Sapphire Zagni

A DOG'S LIFE

I'm madly in love with the poodle
Who lives down the road by the tree,
But I'm only a poor mixed up mongrel
And she don't take no notice of me.
I've seen her give sly little glances
At that spaniel with the long pedigree,
But he's quite enrapt with an Airedale,
And all three of 'em don't speak to me.
I know the Labrador lusts after a Lurcher,
For he once confided in me
Down by the last but one lamp post
Where we'd both paused to have a quick *pee*
Jack Russell just can't make his mind up
If the Peke or the Pom it should be.
While I sit here lovelorn and lonely
My only companion - a flea.
But hang on! Here comes that cute little collie
And doggone it! She's smiling at me.

Edith A Groves

A STRANGE DREAM

He walked alone,
No-one could hear his voice,
And he moved just slightly out of time.
The music from his heart
Filled the sky with excited laughter,
He became close to a girl,
Weak from a troubled world,
But eventually he had to kill her
Out of irresistible cruelty
And the instinct for freedom . . .

160

I awaken from a strange dream,
I am pregnant, with the child's arms outstretched.
He will leave for Montreal this very day.
He stands tall along with the vase beneath the waterwheel.
It's coming through,
It is everything that I could ever fear.

He is lily-white, dark and thin.
An overwhelming rush of light
Came from the depths of my soul
As the swirling wings of the infinite
Dissolved into silence.

I keep him also in my soul.

Cathi Shovlin

HANGING IN SPACE

Blood draining from my face,
a hair-raising stunt if you like,
head yawing to the stars,
trickier than any trick bike.
I bless the providential laws
that keep my feet in place,
safe on Earth's green ceiling,
for my head should be reeling
and I should surely be,
as the sun climbs higher,
more pod-scared than a pea
suffering from claustrophobia.

But I reckon I'm in luck,
there's no nerve inside her,
old Earth she won't buck -
which is just as well,
for sure as hell
I ain't no rodeo rider.

John Ellis

WORLD WAR II AIR RAIDS

Whining aeroplanes, blasting bombs, smouldering smoke,
that make me choke. Beams of light, red, yellow, orange
and white.
Guns are cracking, glass is shattering, flashing searchlights
The droning of a fire brigade, coming to the scene.

I see my eyes fill up with tears, because of loud
bombing rings in my ears. I start choking because of smoke.

Bombs are here, explosives are there,
droning warns us to take care. Help! Help! The people
cry, watching other loved ones die.

If I could wish one wish I say, I wish the war would
end today. But the colours in the sky I see people are
scared just like me.

The crashing and crackling of my friend's house, I just
hope the family got out.
Darkness is back, the streets are black, the fire is high
Tears creep out of my eye. I did have seven friends
now I have six, I stood up and kicked some sticks.

With madness and horror, I scribbled on the side of the
Shelter, hate and fear is back, is here.
I liked that friend, I loved, who cared, but that's not it
Just one little bit.
My life is in this horrid war, the bombing, the friends,
I can't take much more.

Laura Godtschalk (10)

FRIENDS

I used to feel a little sad
But now I'm feeling more than glad
That I've met John

He lost his wife, she's now at rest
My husband died, was for the best
Before I met John

He seems to like my company
Pops round to have a cup of tea
'Can I come in?' says John

Days were lonely on my own
Apart from chatting on the phone
Before I knew John

And though the family were beside me
They couldn't always stay to guide me
So I welcomed John

It's nice to have a friend nearby
To share a smile or little cry
Sometimes with John

We go down to the town to shop
I'll see a friend, we always stop
Now everyone's met John

I've had my share of sorrow
Waiting for a new tomorrow
It's better now with John

And so whatever lies ahead
We'll stand each other in good stead
Good health long life to John
And Phyllis too, says John.

Joan C Phipps

THE MAIDEN

The cottage door stood open
To the beauty of the world.
It revealed a pretty maiden
With hair so neatly curled.
Her apron was a dancing to
The breezes in the air
And the flowers in the garden
Seemed to be aware
That a nature loving being
Had her basket come to fill
So they opened upwards to the sun
Who shone with a goodwill
The birds up in the tree tops
Sang their songs in glee
And the maiden said, 'This beauty
God has lent to me.
I will feed the birds each morning
And will treat the flowers with care
From the little snow white daisies
To the lilies blooming rare.'
The maid fulfilled her promise
And pleased the Lord so well
That he carried her to Heaven,
Happy there with him to dwell.

Joan Britton

LONELINESS

Loneliness is . . .
      A thousand words unsaid
      Behind the barrier of your eyes.
      A cold space in your bed
      The first dead leaf as summer dies.

Loneliness is . . .
>
> Standing by the sea.
> Footsteps in a night street tapping.
> A closing door, a turning key.
> The new dress unworn in its wrapping.

Loneliness is . . .
>
> People's laughter overhearing
> The insistent whispers in your mind.
> Car tail lights disappearing
> A remembered room you left behind.

Loneliness is . . .
>
> A thousand steps upon a shore.
> The memory that stings
> The roads of time. The waiting for.
> The pendulum that swings.

Hazel Brown

EARTHLY WHISTLE

It was a summer's day.
The sky was silent,
No voices. The roads a desolate pilot.

Just a soft whistle.
The meadows breathing,
A village empty, the dead were waking!

Walking the hills
listening to the earth.
No sign of the heart of nature's birth.

Embrace and caress
these fading delights.
Walk endlessly to the beautification of night.

Mat Duggan

FROST

I looked, I stared at a jewel bright,
Not sure my eyes were seeing right,
It sparkled, bright blue, red and green,
The loveliest prize I'd ever seen.
With fire it danced, it shone, it gleamed,
Beauty of which I'd often dreamed,
With hand outstretched I bent to hold
This gem of wealth, as yet untold.
Treasure here, my own to view
I looked again and then I knew . . .

No jewel this that shone so clear,
No fortune here I'd felt so near,
But sun and ice together met -
A diamond, there in winter set.
I looked again, in wonder feeling,
It glittered there, bright facets gleaming,
But as I gazed, the warming sun
Shone down, and then my dream was done
For as I watched, it slipped away
Its beauty gone, but memories stay.

Iris Lampert

NUNNEY CASTLE SOMERSETSHIRE
(Engraved by J Grieg after a drawing by P Crocker
for the Antiquarian and Topographical Cabinet.)

Six square inches of fine engraving
Filched from an antiquarian book.

For two minute horses and one tired rider
A pause in the summer afternoon,
While one mount drinks from the moat.

A four-square keep with four squat towers,
Had been a shell for two hundred years,

166

A Civil War arsenal, fired by the lantern
Dropped by a drunken soldier.

It was bought for pence twenty years ago,
For reasons sentimental,
In a dusky junk shop,
Recalling a starry summer night
When, like silly children, for a dare,
They climbed the padlocked gate
Under the moon's eye,
And lost their shyness
Within the embrace of those sturdy walls.

Pamela Wiles

EAT YER 'EART OUT, PAMMIE!

Move over, Pam - I'm comin' through,
An I could be the same as you
With me 'ouse laid out in all the Sunday sups. -
Though I wouldn't live in Weston,
'Cos I'd 'ave to keep me vest on
With that chilly breeze a'rattlin' through me cups!

But I couldn't 'ack the grammar.
English mangled with an 'ammer.
What 'appens to the aitches that you drop?
Do they all go up the 'oover
Or d'you buy an aitch remover?
Would I find it at me local 'ardware shop?

I wouldn't be a threat to you
Cos I don't write the way you do -
And I really wouldn't want yer lovely 'ome.
But keep yer eye out for the name,
As I try to stake me claim
In the market for the funny little pome . . .

Debbie Lyne

THOUGHTS OF THE LOVELY MAY

In a room, buried in thoughts was I,
I'll never forget those days even if time dies,
We all were together having fun,
going for picnics and enjoying the warm sun.
Time was passing rather fast,
I didn't have any idea whether these joys would last
having fun was all our concern,
together we had lots of things to learn.
Something happened! What? I had been distracted
by the noise in the house,
Something might have scared the family, maybe a mouse.
I looked at the ceiling,
This time I had an odd feeling,
Will we all meet again?
Will the joys come again?
I suppose no, it was only a thought
Something at which I had to laugh a lot.
Those days were the best of all
It was much fun, when we visited the shopping mall.
I'll never forget a single day,
When together we enjoyed the lovely days of May.

Bianca Daniel (13)

UNTITLED

Many thoughts kept hidden
Many thoughts expressed
Some we have to write about -
and so doing put to rest

Anita Heap

LOST AT SEA

To the beggar a few pence;
Unfolded amongst solitude
Wallowed in waters of recompense,

Glistening as paper rain,
Shackled to the castle walls alight,
Mortal fruit at the table wept,
As her maiden voyage,
Shipwrecked;

Sailors yearning sorrow
As were the waves,
Trestled in locks of golden honey spun,
When had your life begun?

As I wallow in waters of recompense,
Unfold my solitude
As to the beggar a few pence;

Glistening now as paper rain,
Sailors yearn mortal fruit,
At the table shipwrecked they wept;
As waves,
Trestled in locks of golden honey spun,
When had your life begun?

Spindled in the web you had spun;
Cast the net unto the shore,
Waves floundering set you free,
For me, I ask nothing more.

A Angel

169

THE ANGEL ISLE

Through purple heather moorlands,
My weary feet have trod.
The bracken heaths of golden brown,
reflect the work of Gods.
The blissful summer hamlets, delight the sage's eye.
In plush green forest clearings, my body yearns to lie.
This island of the angels,
Britain is her name,
Shall hold my heart forever,
I her wondrous Chattelaine.
Oh how I love this splendorous land,
With her perfect warm embrace.
The beauty of this Virgin Isle,
Shall challenge any grace.
Oh misty hillside winter,
and scorching harvest field,
preserve thy charm forever.
Then cold grey hearts will yield,
to you, my darling homeland,
Whose seas rage wild and blue.
And though this humble poet may travel,
his heart remains with you.

A M Dyer

STOP THIS CRUELTY

What is this world coming to,
See the animals in the zoo,
They all deserve their freedom,
It is still their kingdom.

Watch the fox, trying to run,
The hunters chase him just for fun,
Soon they trap him underground,
Only to end his life, torn apart by the hound.

All over the world, people are the same,
Haven't they got any shame?
Where the cold winds blow,
See the seals in the snow,
Such beautiful creatures, so young and pure,
All they want is their fur,
Soon they are hacked to death,
A life, just for the sake of wealth.

They say, 'Charity begins at home,' so does cruelty,
A little puppy, what a novelty,
It soon becomes an unwanted present,
Neglected, and forgotten, so innocent.

Yet all God's creatures,
Can give us so much pleasure,
They don't deserve to die, or be neglected,
Together, we will fight to have them protected,
One day we will put a *Stop to this Cruelty*.

H Philp

INFORMATION

We hope you have enjoyed reading this book - and that you will continue to enjoy it in the coming years.

If you like reading and writing poetry drop us a line, or give us a call, and we'll send you a free information pack.

Write to

Poetry Now Information
1-2 Wainman Road
Woodston
Peterborough
PE2 7BU